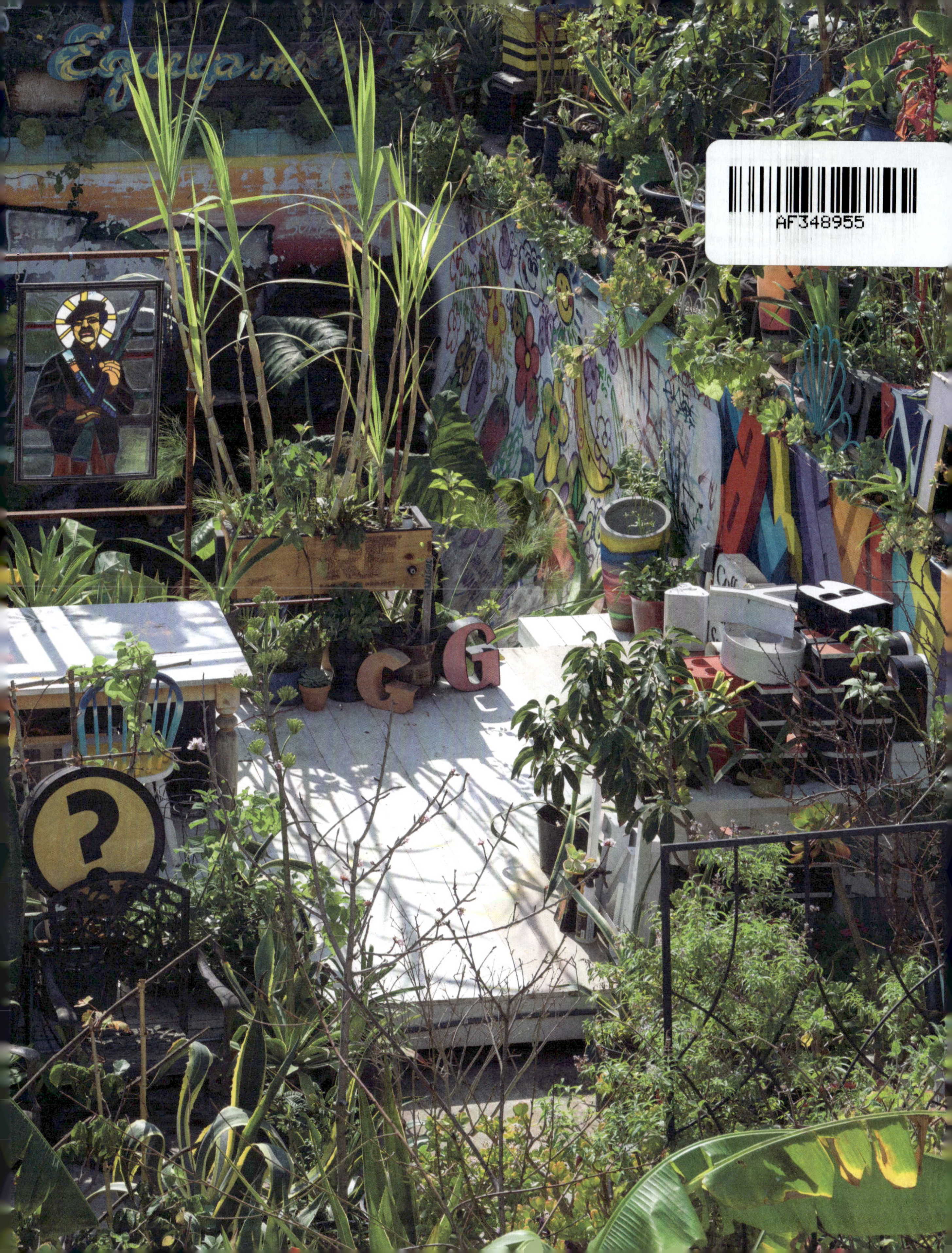

Equipam
?
G G

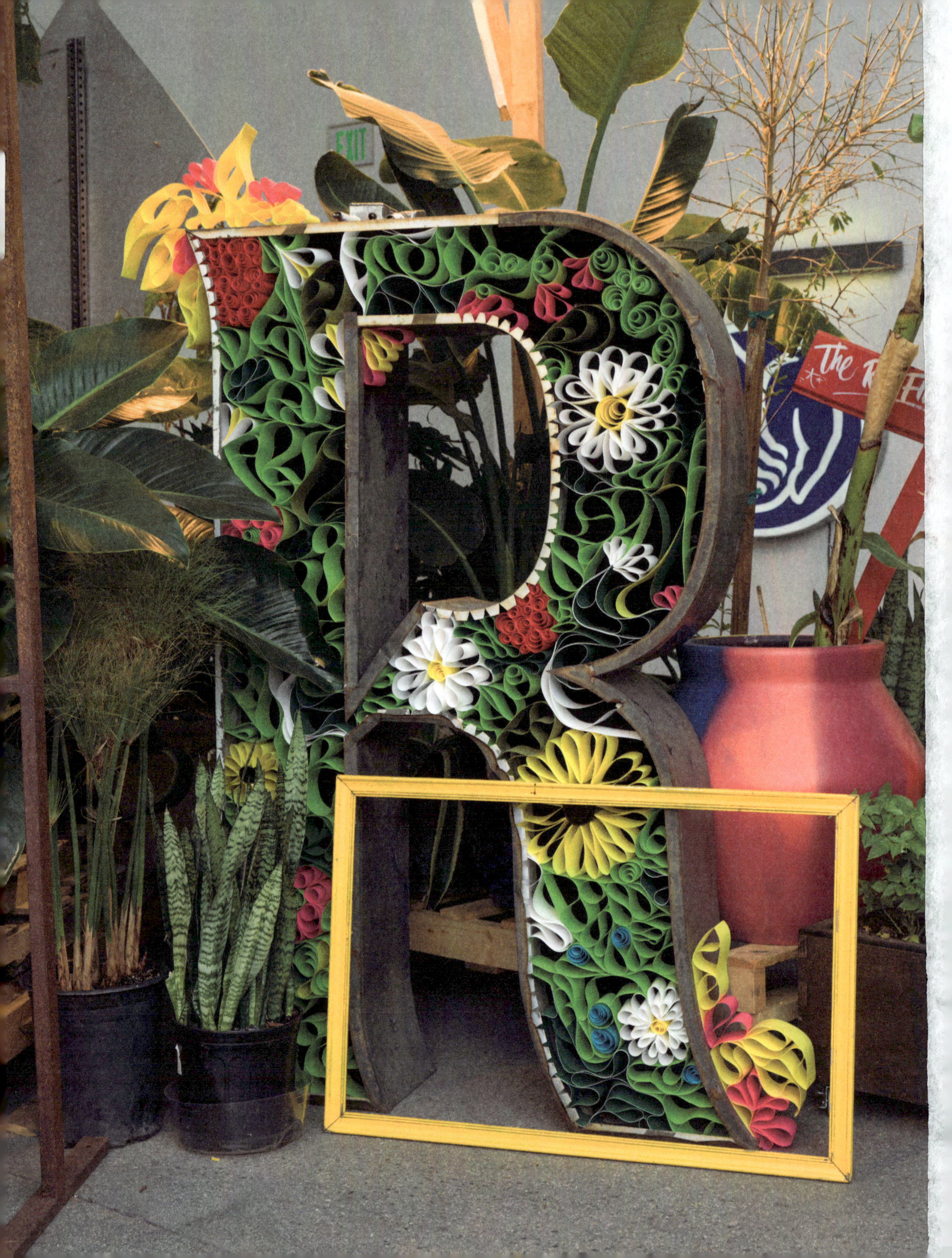

EXIT
The R

Ron Finley

The Gangsta Gardener

HAMMER MUSEUM
UNIVERSITY OF CALIFORNIA,
LOS ANGELES

DELMONICO BOOKS · D.A.P.
NEW YORK

FOREWORD

The Hammer Museum is proud to present the work of Ron Finley, a visionary designer, horticulturalist, and artist who has changed the perception of concrete spaces using only a seed and a shovel. Known as the "Gangsta Gardener," Finley's transformative work in South Central Los Angeles has redefined what it means to grow food and regenerate communities. His gardening initiatives through the Ron Finley Project reclaim and redesign neglected urban spaces such as abandoned lots, shelters, traffic medians, and curb strips. This enables Finley to bring fresh, organic produce to food deserts, while also sparking local and international movements toward food sovereignty and communal reciprocity.

In 2009, Finley began planting vegetables, fruit trees, and vibrant flowers in the parkways around his neighborhood, beautifying barren spaces into green sanctuaries. When the city fined him for gardening without a permit, Finley fought back and ultimately changed the city's gardening jurisdiction on parkways, starting a food revolution in South Central and beyond. "I wanted butterflies and hummingbirds. I wanted something pretty, like amaryllis and agapanthus, and I wanted it to smell like jasmine, juniper, mint, and orange blossoms," Finley recalls, describing the potential he envisioned in urban spaces.

Ron Finley's pop-up garden at the Hammer, *Grounded* (2024), reflects his belief that creativity and art can flourish anywhere—not just in studios, but in the very ground beneath our feet. The installation invites visitors to step into a living, breathing extension of Finley's vision, where gardens become spaces of connection, learning, and empowerment. As part of the *Breath(e): Toward Climate and Social Justice* exhibition, this garden comes to life through a series of workshops led by Finley and a group of local artists, activists, and teachers. These hands-on community-led sessions explore topics such as transplanting, natural dyeing using flowers such as marigolds, making tortillas from traditional heirloom corn, and regenerative gardening practices. Also on display within the museum's galleries, Finley's *Urban Weaponry Project, Weapons of Mass Creation* (2018–) installation features fifty shovels decorated and painted by local artists. With this project, Finley encourages underserved communities to take charge of their own self-determination, using shovels as an antidote to the oppressive designs of urban infrastructure.

We are deeply grateful to Ron Finley for sharing his invaluable contributions to environmental activism, social justice, and the arts. Featuring his practice within the Hammer's *Breath(e)* exhibition acts as a reminder that radical transformation often begins in unexpected places and that the act of growing—whether plants, ideas, or communities—holds the power to inspire, heal, and reimagine the world around us.

— Glenn Kaino and Mika Yoshitake

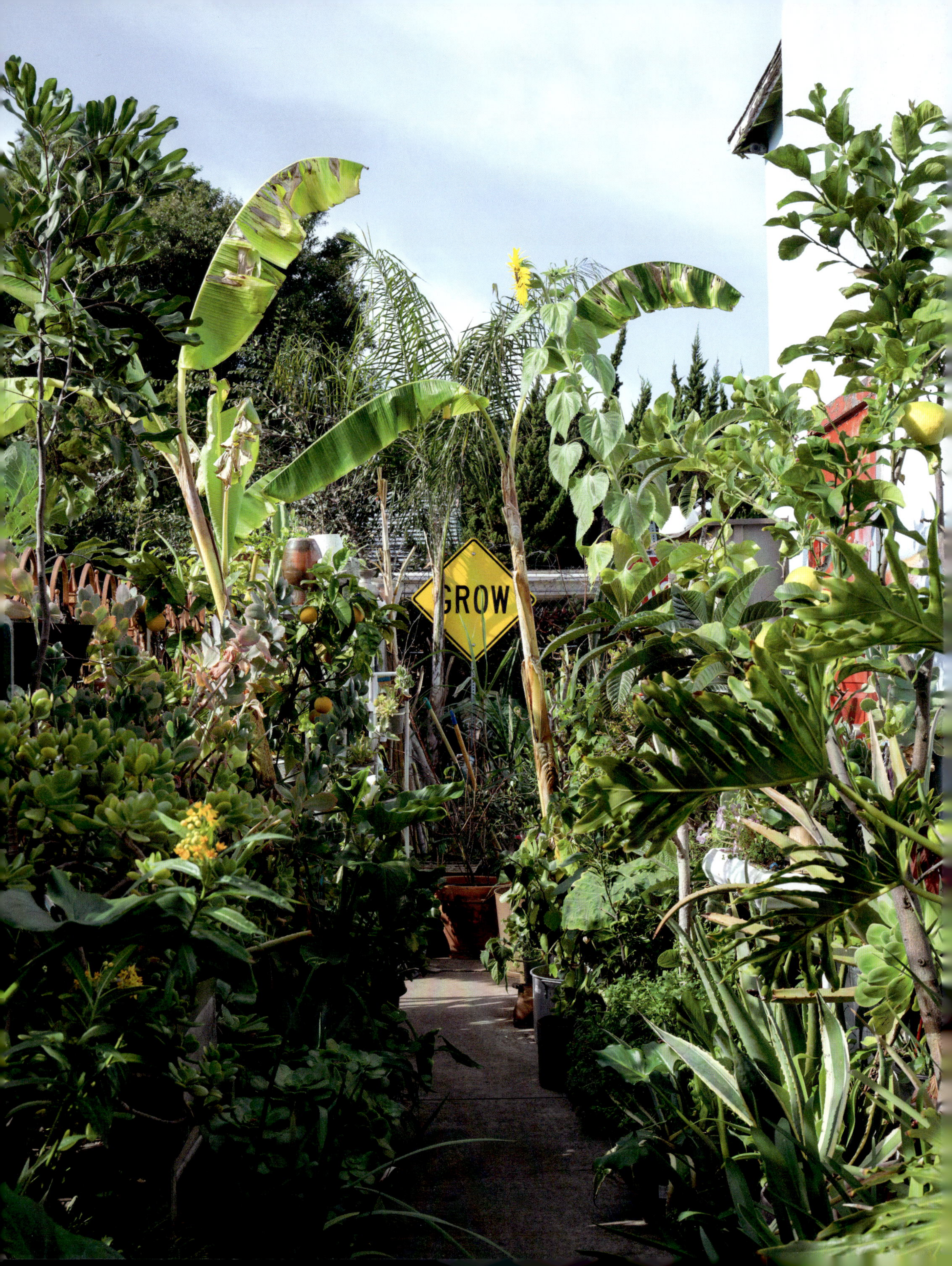
GROW

WHY I DO WHAT I DO AND WHY YOU SHOULD DO WHAT I DO TOO!

Ron Finley

Why I Do What I Do and Why You Should Do What I Do Too!

I do what I do because I care for you and this planet too.

We all should care, so we can breathe healthy fresh Air.

We must stray away from how we are treating the world today, cus if we continue on this way I'm not sure we will see a brighter day.

It is imperative and you, Yes, YOU must be inclined to untwine, re-design and retrofit your mind. Because we have to re-think what we are leaving behind. For we are the future Ancestors of our time.

Plant some trees and collect the leaves. This builds soil. For you to plant more trees.

No one ever taught me to see the power in one seed. A forest is contained in a single seed.

This is a powerful lesson for us all to realize.

Biomimicry Is what you need to be doing. Practicing this will let you see the magic of a leaf.

And Compost! Compost!! COMPOST!!! One simple act that can change our planet.

Pages 4–19:
Ron Finley Project Garden,
Los Angeles

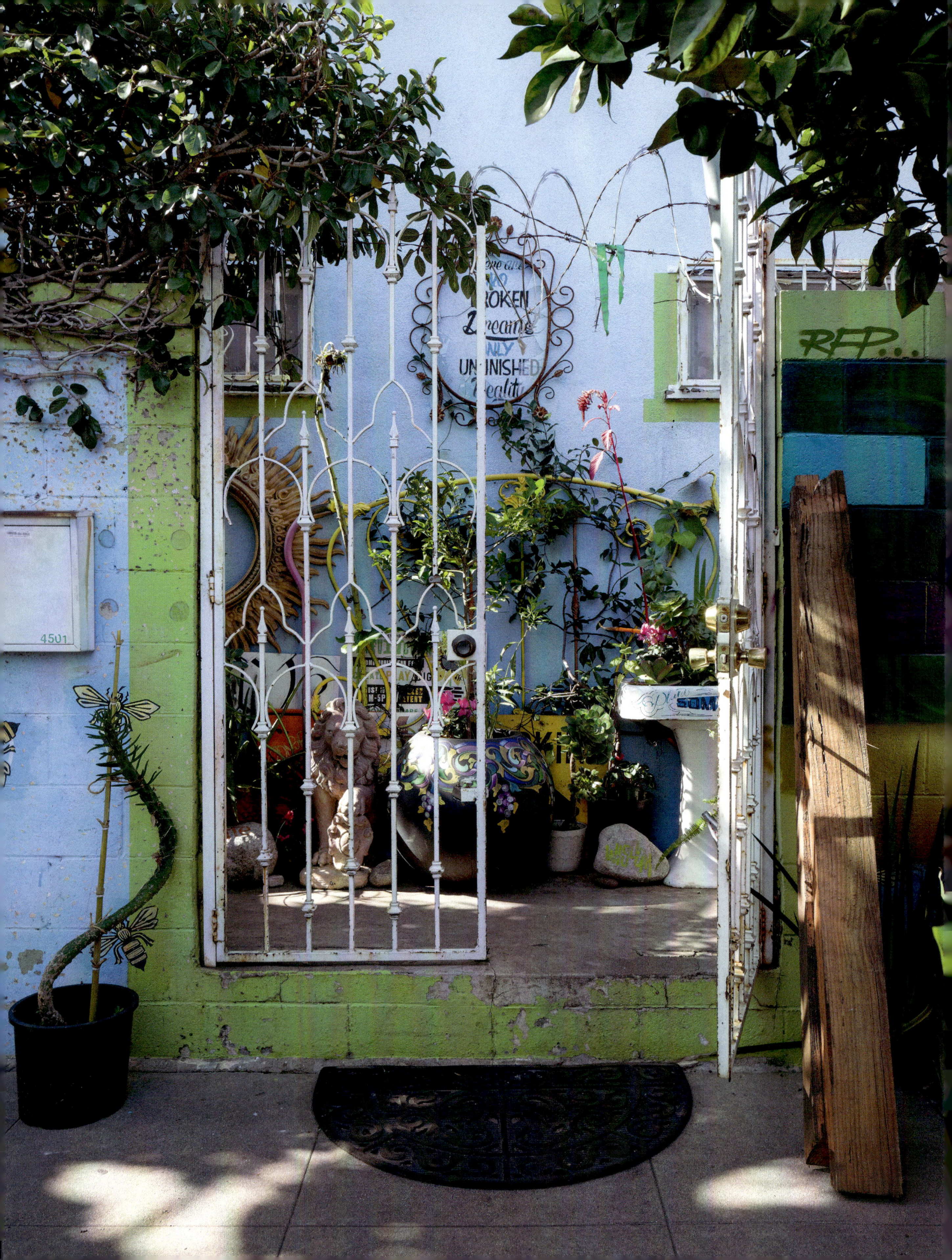
4501
BROKEN
Dreams
UNFINISHED
Reality
REP...

Why I Do What I Do and Why You Should Too.

Because we all have a vital role to play in reversing climate change.

You can sit around and be tranquilized, neutralized, paralyzed, horrified, terrorized and derealized. Or you can get yo ass up and do something about it.

How did we get to this place in time? Man's need for greed. And now they want to own all the seed.

I often pray that the forces at play that lead us astray would just fade away like a gray winter's day.

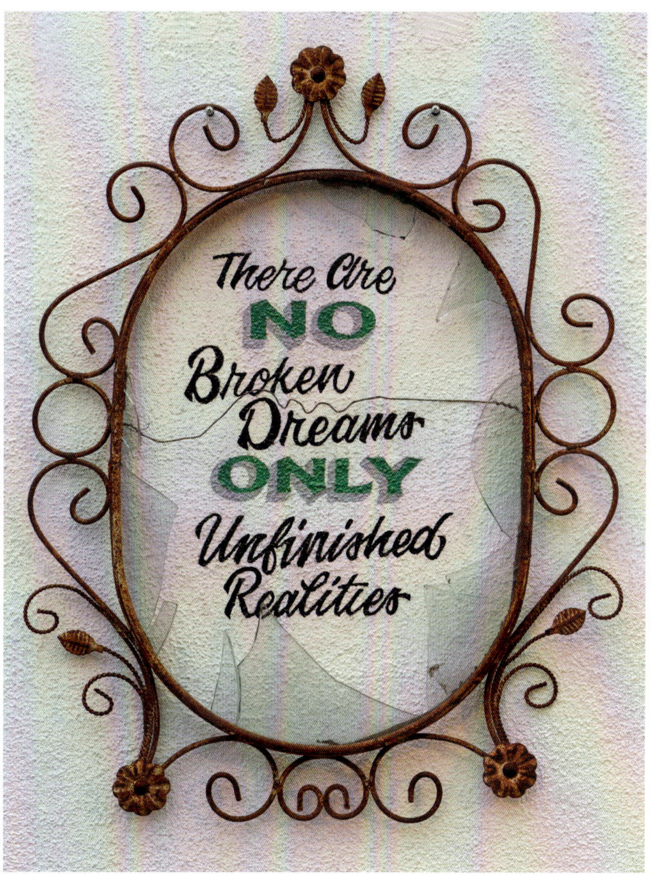

Why I Do What I Do and Why You Can Too

We planted a tree and the so-called powers that be wanted to arrest me and destroy the tree!

You see just how silly they can be? I'm still trying to see why it would be necessary for me to be validated by these so-called powers that be?

Growing your own food is a human right! Or it should be!

Being healthy is a form of resistance. Swords to Plowshares.

Let your shovel be your Weapon of Choice to change the system of food inequality.

Raise Your Spades!

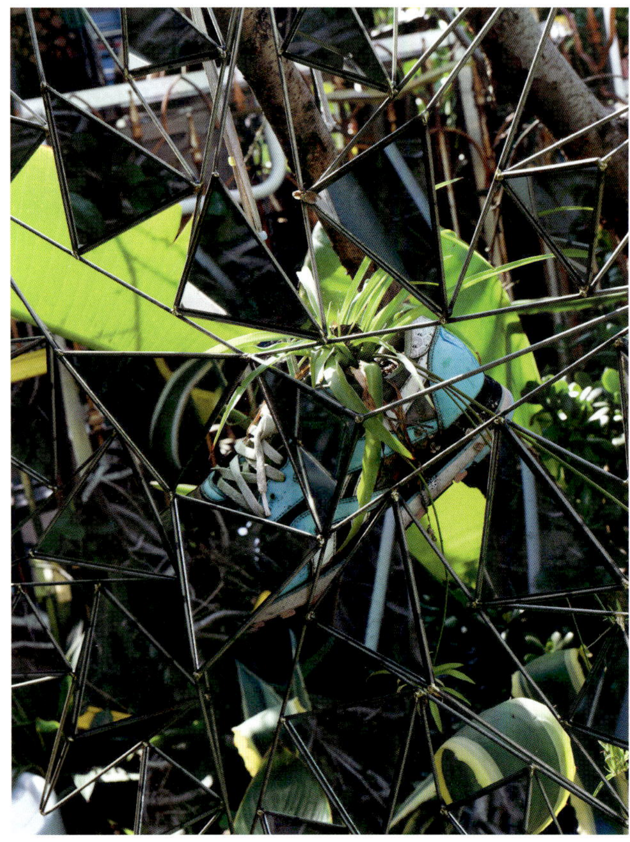

                    RON FINLEY

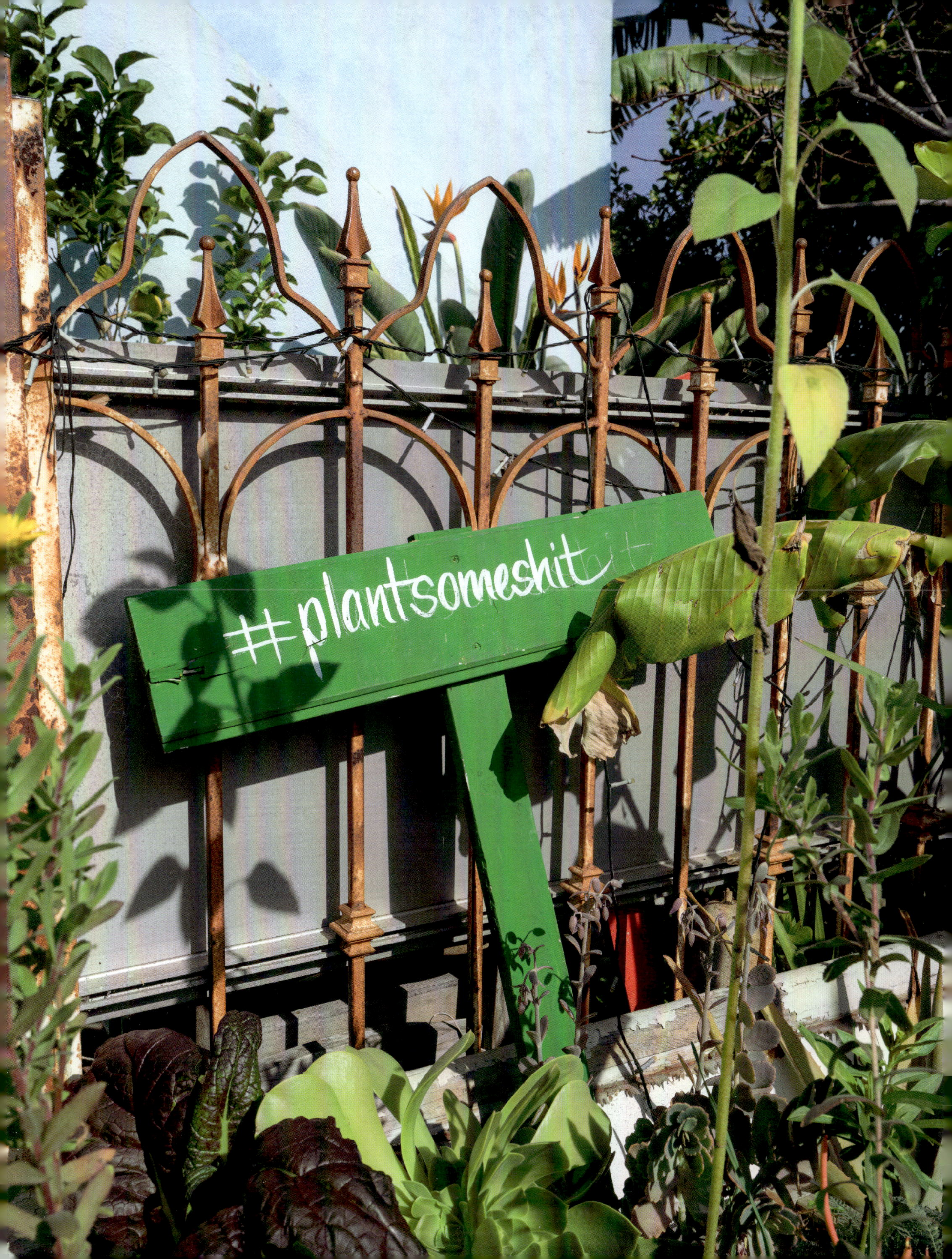
#plantsomeshit

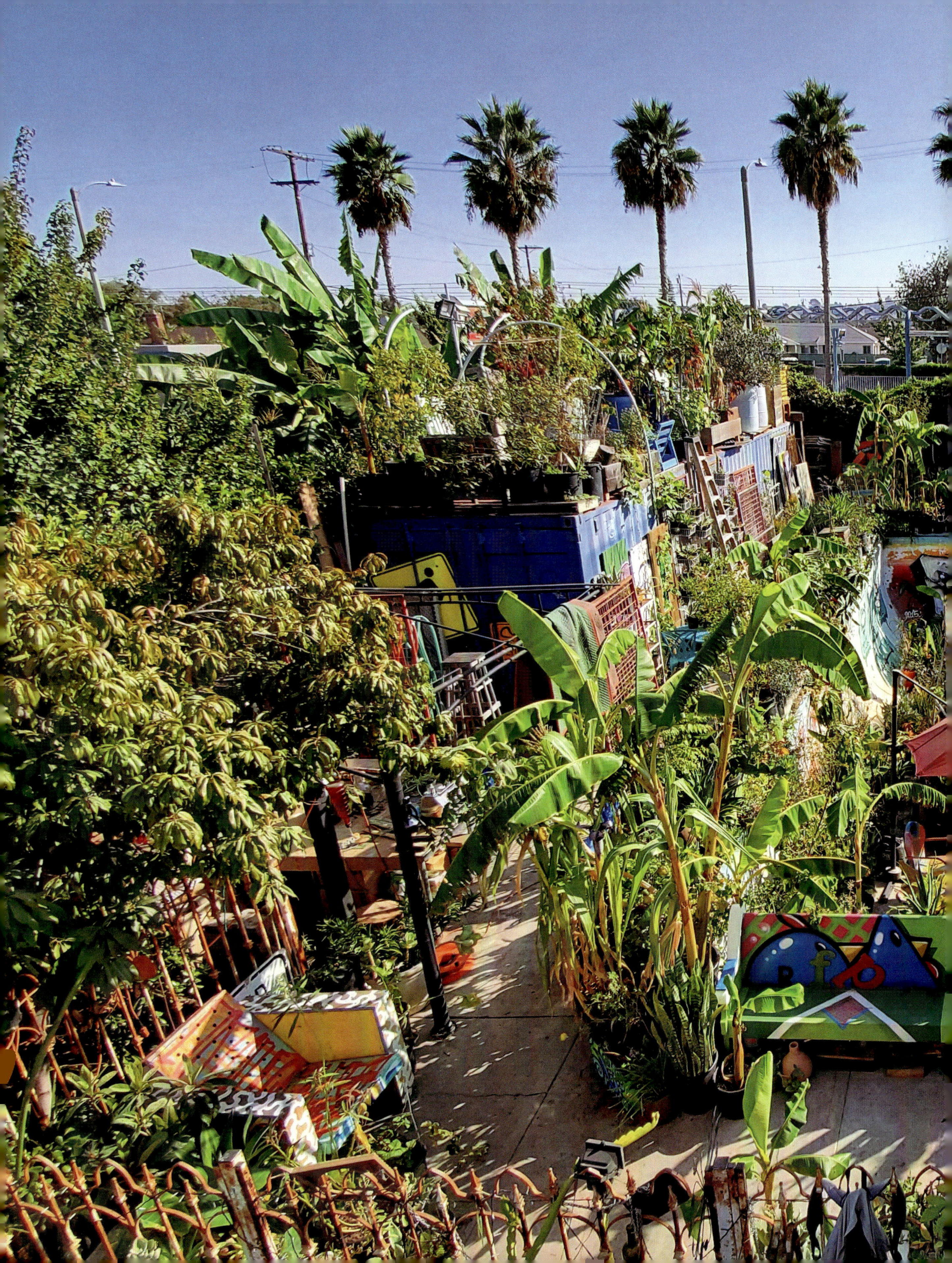

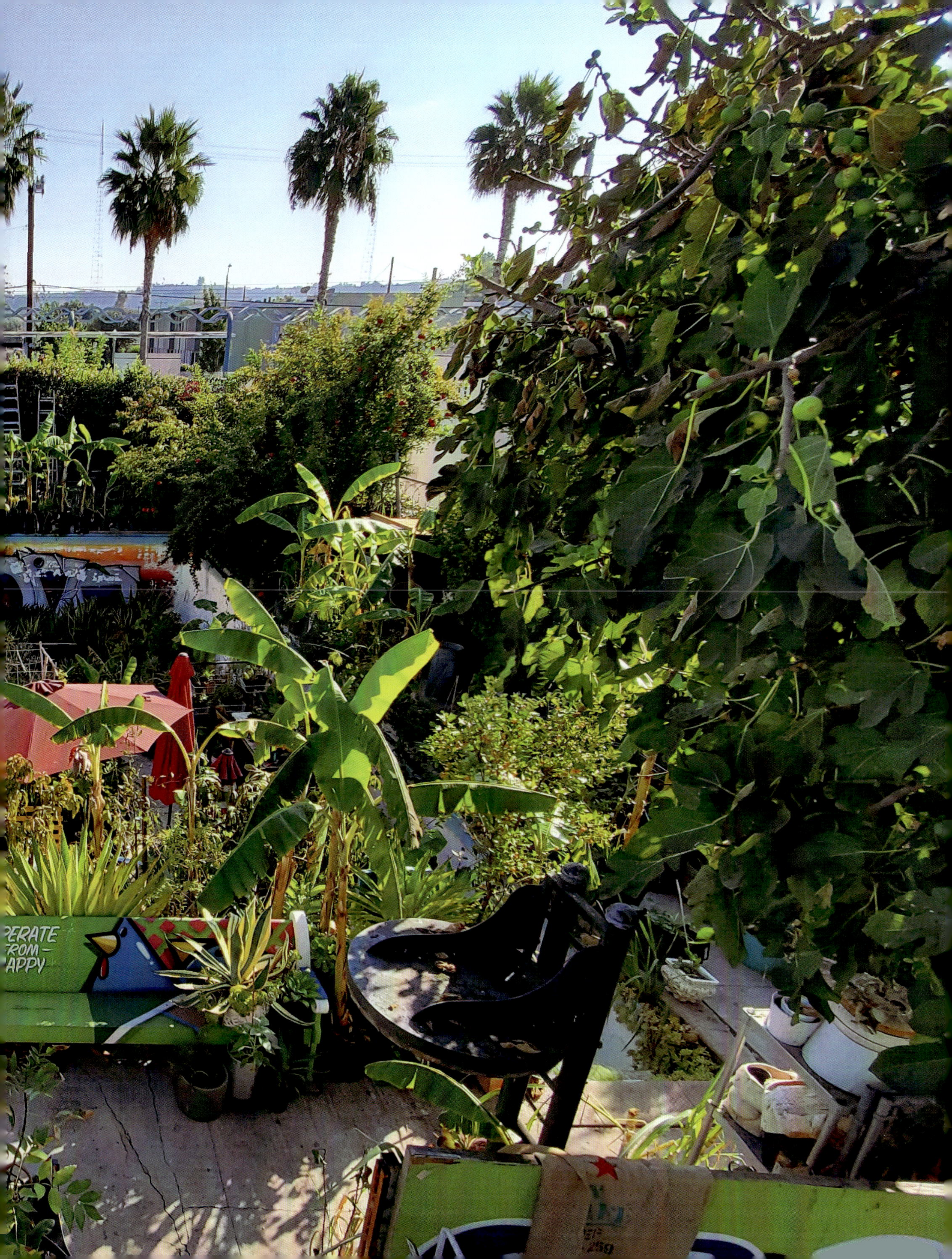
PERATE
FROM—
APPY

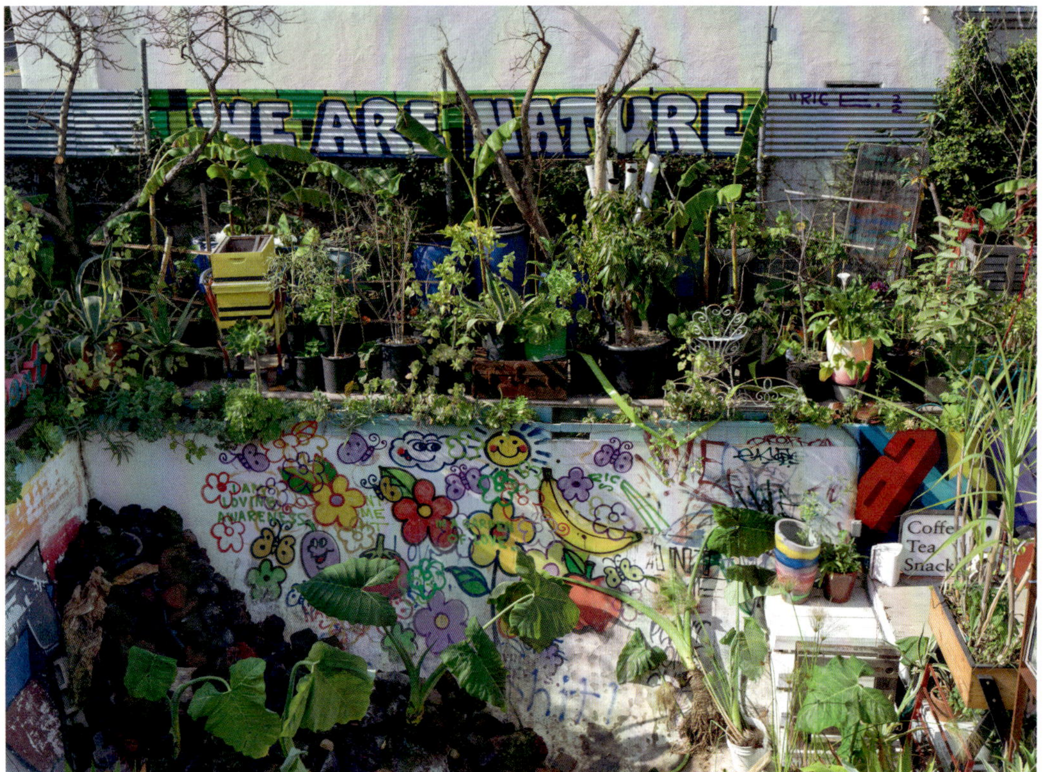

Why I Do What I Do and So Can You Too

Built on a foundation of Slavery, Humiliation, Castration, Mutilation, Miseducation, Colonization, & now Gentrification.

How can I trust you when I've witnessed the thangs you consciously do? Then you show little to no remorse or attempt to reverse the course, sorry I meant curse of these actions.

Now you want to remove us from the books so that it looks like we never existed.

So now what it will be is your real-fake His-Story.

Just let us Breathe.

They think that we are so naive and easy to deceive. Because they always have new tricks up their dirty ass sleeves that we have to unweave.

Just let us Breathe.

Let us conceive and believe that we are just as valuable as you are.

The only thing I want to see hanging from a tree is Food!

. . . or maybe a swing, yeah maybe a swing.

Why I Do What I Do

No access to healthy food is a byproduct of institutionalized racism.

They say that they want our children to compete, but they constantly give them poisonous shit to eat.

Just another way to lead our children astray.

Change culture. Change values. Educate to collaborate. Build places with beautiful safe spaces. And you will see silly smiling faces.

Education not indoctrination. Teach the children just how brilliant they are. Teach them who they are. Not who you want them to be. No child is standard. So fuck your standardized education. Teach them the way they learn. Not how you teach. Show them that their Imagination is the greatest, most powerful nation. And that nothing has more value than them.

I want people to stop and see the Beauty and the Alchemy.

I want children to witness the intricate design of a Butterfly's chrysalis and the elaborate structure of a Dragonfly's wing. Marvel at the beauty of a Hummingbird. Smell the blossom of a fresh Casablanca Lily. They should know the difference between a Tomato and a Peach. Kale and Collard Greens. Radishes, Carrots, and Beets.

I want them to taste the flavor of a Mulberry right off the tree.

I want them to have a tree full of Apples in their front yard.

This will show them abundance and the resources around them every day, and what a seed can do.

This is fundamental to humanity.

It's Like the OG Mr. Paris in Jackson, Miss. would tell me, *"Finley, If You Can't Feed Yourself, You Can't Free YourSelf!"* And We Not Free!

Gardening is the gateway drug to humanity. Because that's what it's about. Us being humane to one another.

Gardening lets you know what true value is. You can't eat diamonds. . .

Gardens make you stop and realize just how magical this ball really is that we're floating on in outer space.

Gardening = Freedom

Real G's Grow Food

I know this sounds like some Hippy shit, but some of the Hippies had it right.

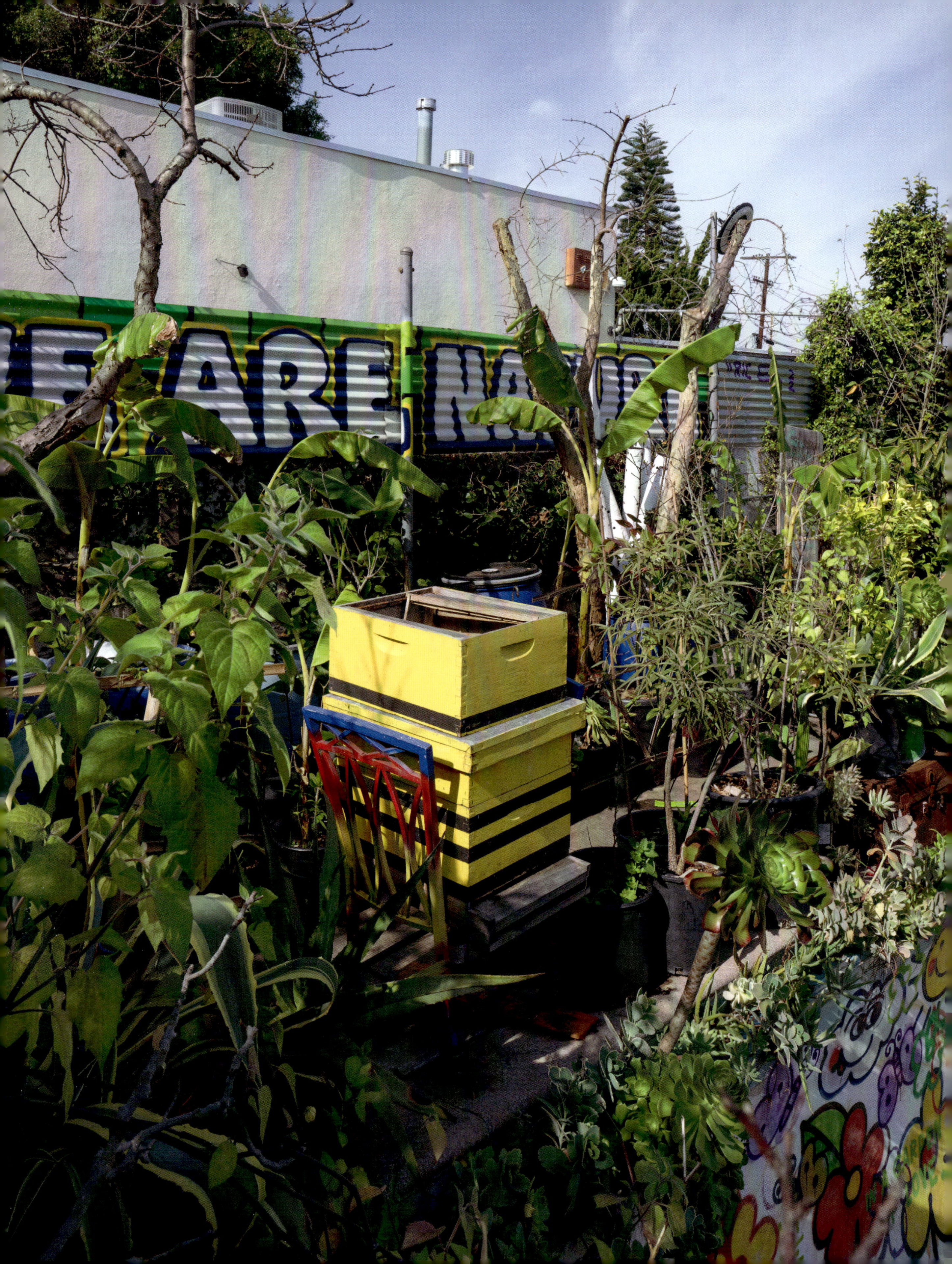
ARE NA

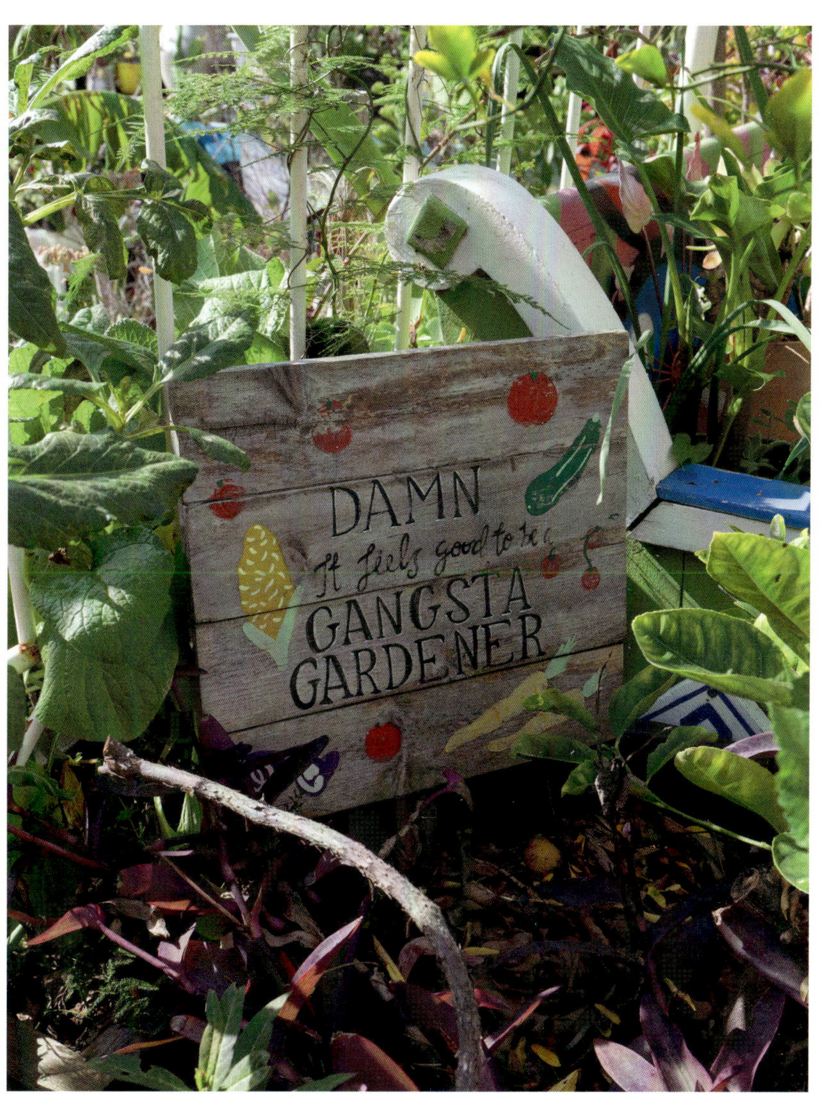

DAMN
It feels good to be a
GANGSTA
GARDENER

Why I Do What I Do and Why Don't You

Do it For YourSelf!

Do it For Culture.

Do it For Knowledge.

Do it For Yourstory.

Do it For Your Family.

Do it For the Animals.

Do it For your Health.

Do it for the Planet.

Do it for the Now.

Do it for the Future.

Do it For LoVe.

People over money.

Systems must be Reevaluated

Remodeled & Reengineered,

Let's Rethink Possibilities.

Reclaim, Recycle, Repurpose Our Lives and Our Resources.

Instead of discarding everything.

Reestablish Community & Reinvigorate Neighborhoods

Renew Purpose, Renew Passion.

Let's Reshape & Reconfigure.

Recover, Regenerate, Revitalize our health and wellness

Restore the Soil.

Resuscitate, Revive, Re-awaken Our Planet

Let's Renovate & Rehabilitate this whole Fucked up

System. . . .

I planted a Garden and All Hell Broke Loose. . . .

P.S. 4 U academics eye know the structure is not right. I know there are probably misspelled words, the punctuation may not be right. Who gives a fuck? I don't, so get over it.

Go Plant some SHIT!!!

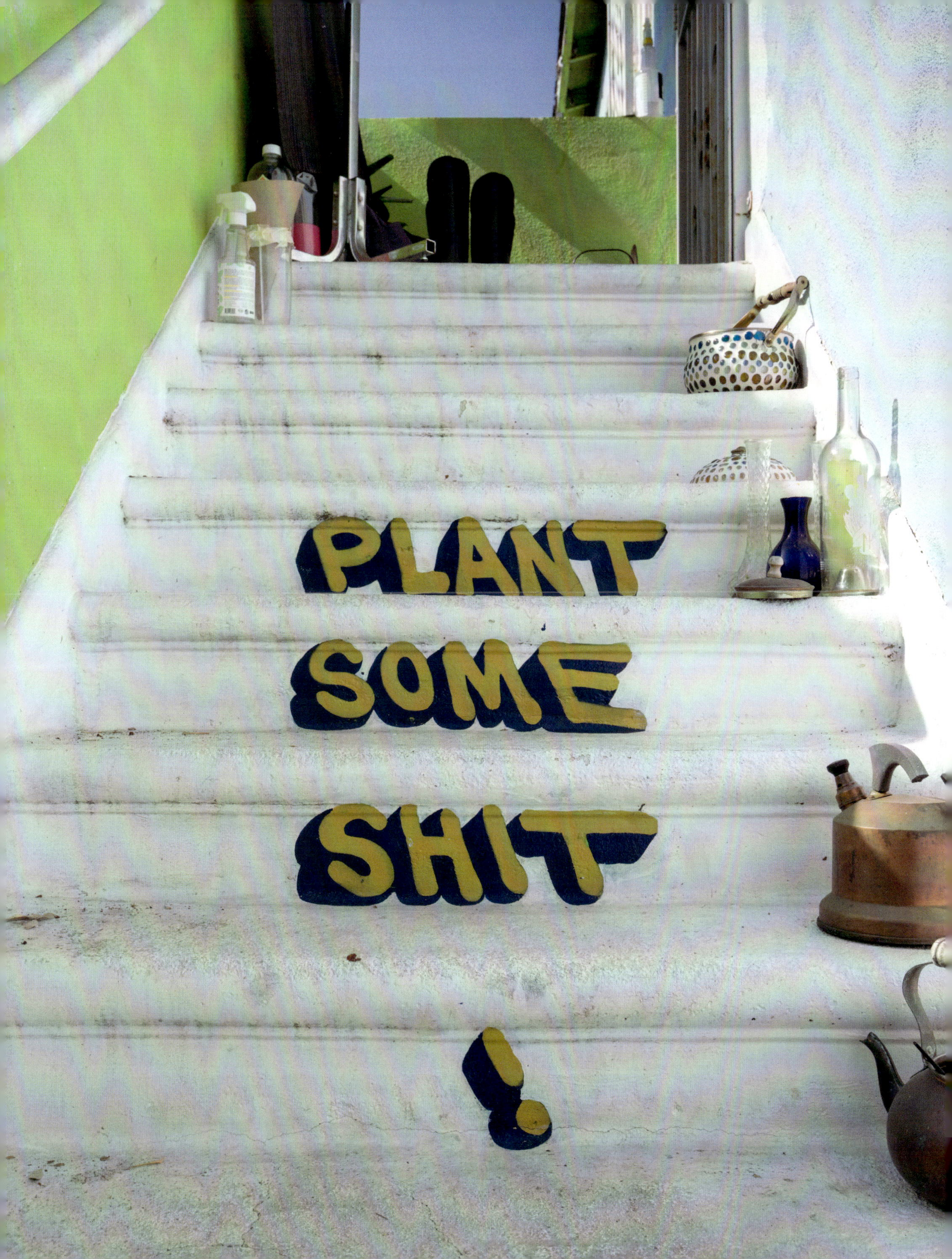
PLANT
SOME
SHIT
!

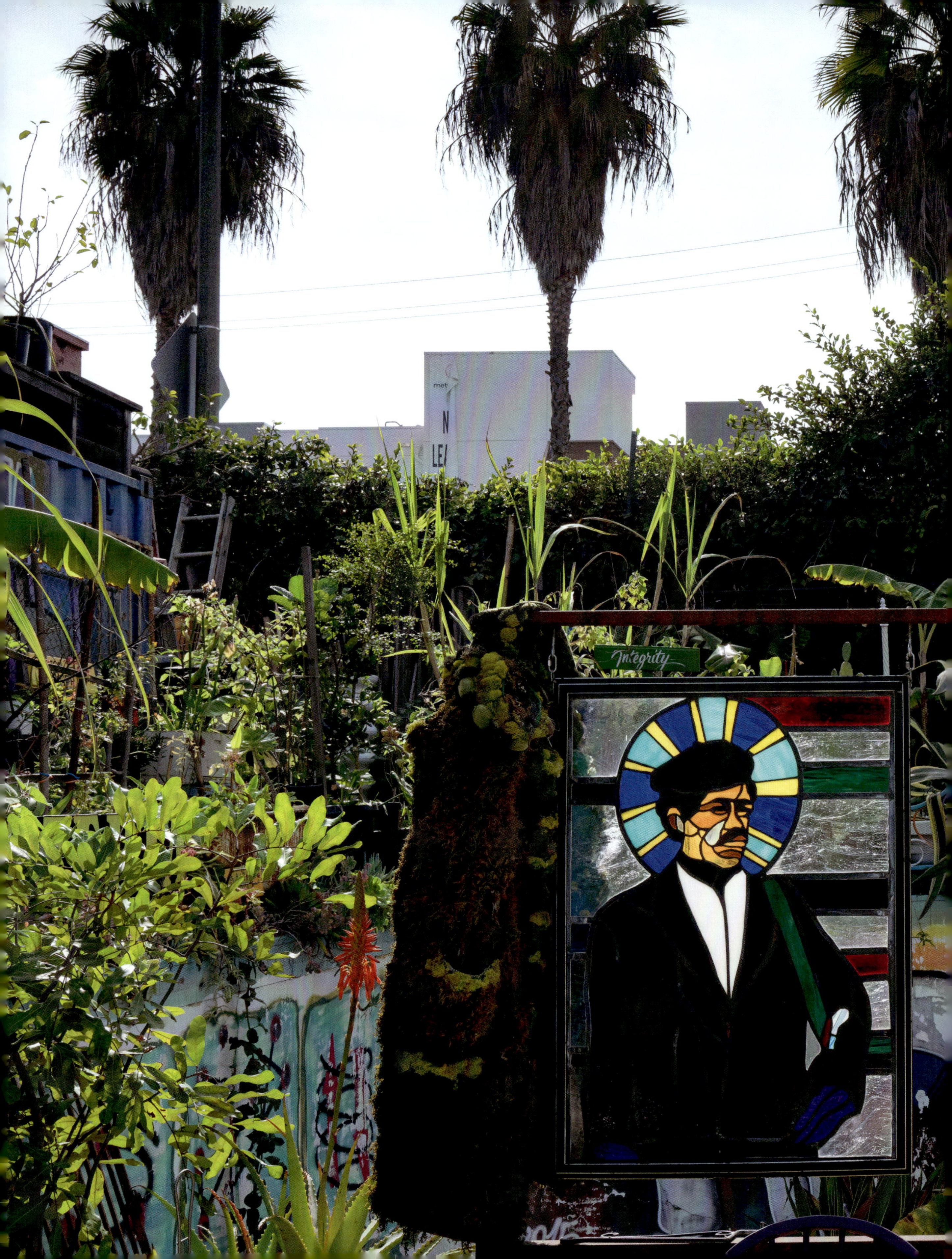
met
N
LEA
Integrity

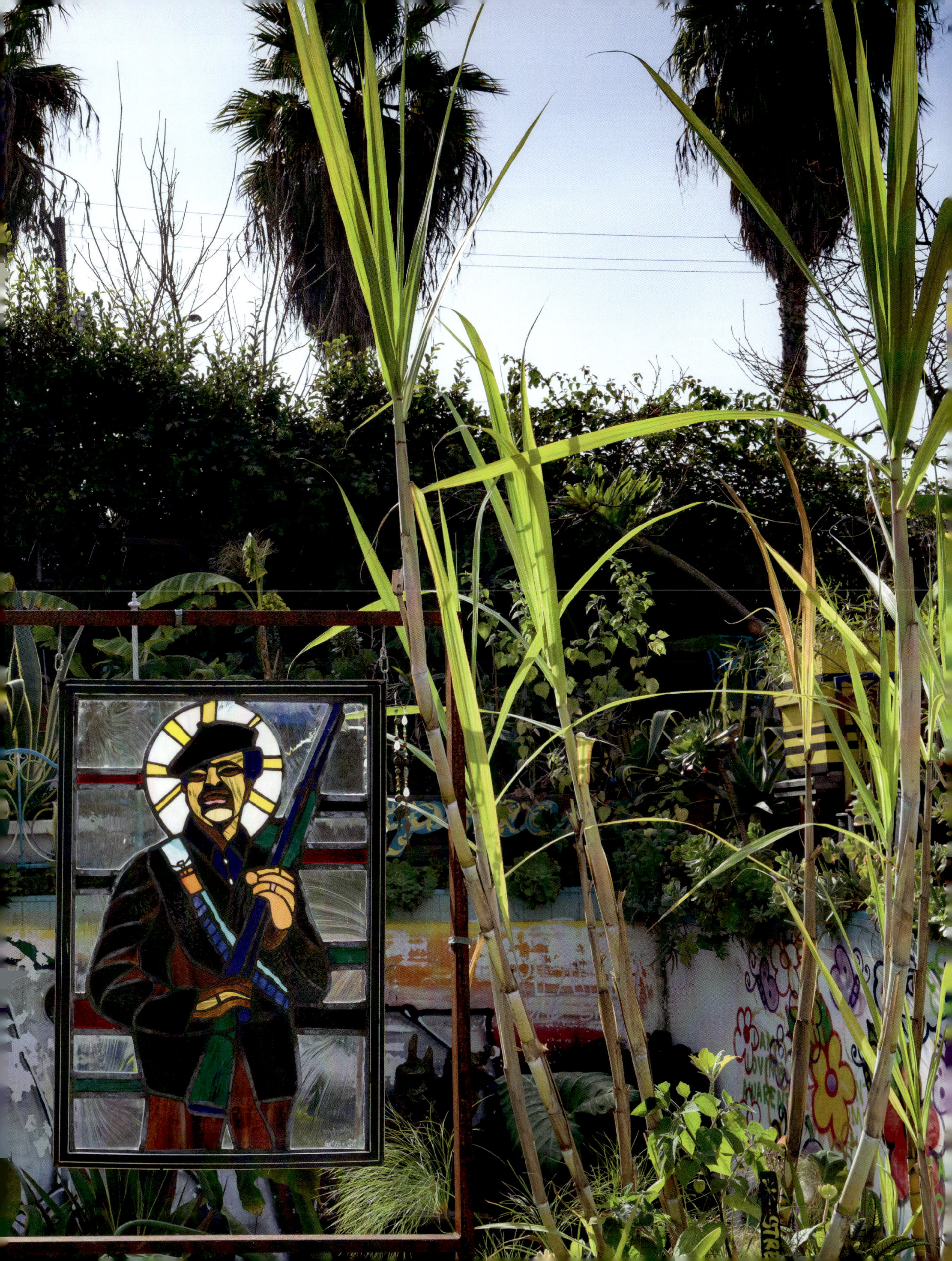

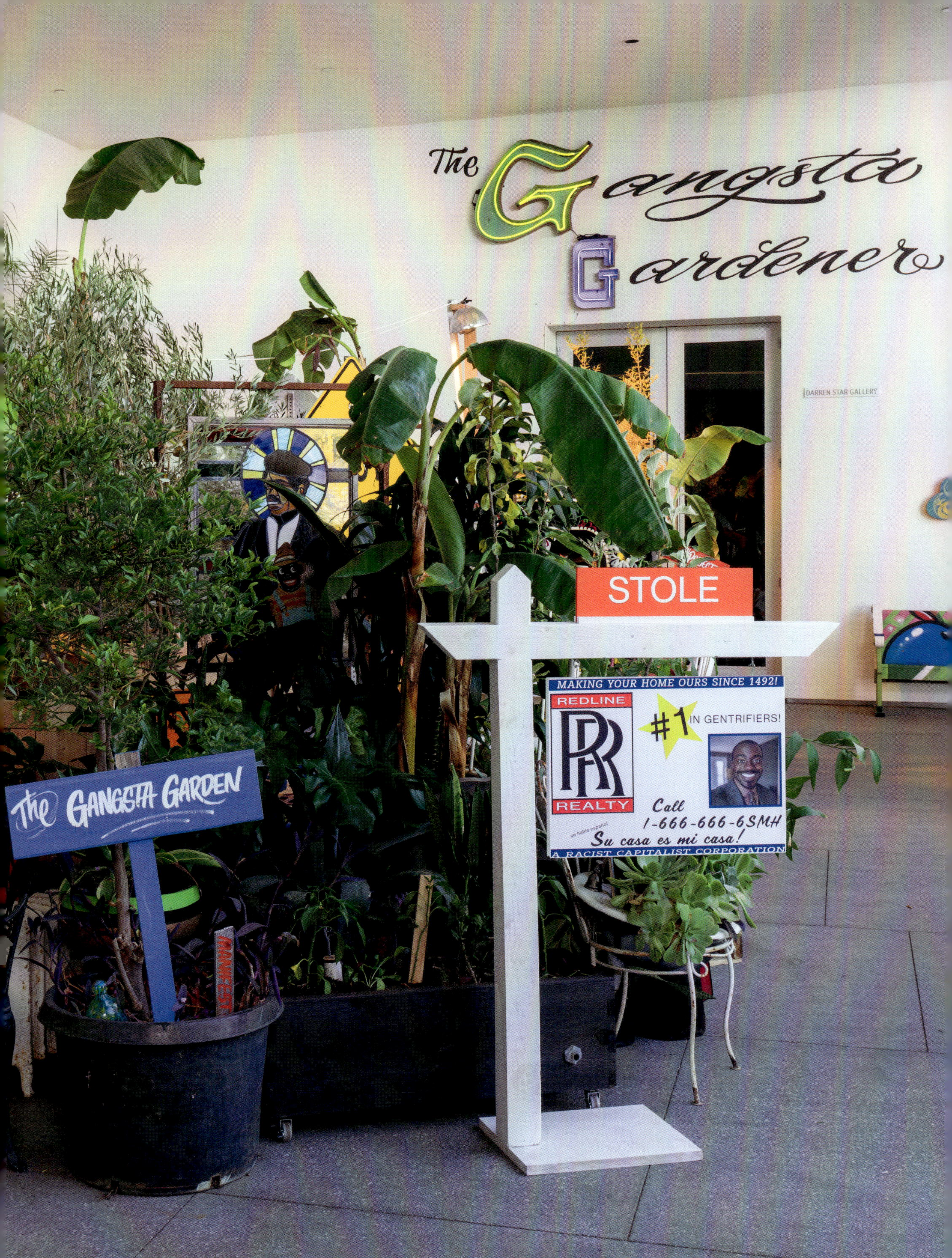
The Gangsta Gardener
DARREN STAR GALLERY
STOLE
The Gangsta Garden
MAKING YOUR HOME OURS SINCE 1492!
REDLINE
RR
REALTY
#1 IN GENTRIFIERS!
se habla español
Su casa es mi casa!
Call
1-666-666-6SMH
A RACIST CAPITALIST CORPORATION

GROUNDED (2024)

With the commissioned work *Grounded*, Finley brings his urban gardening practice to the Hammer Museum, creating a green, nourishing respite on the museum's terrace in emulation of his own extraordinary garden. Both sites include vegetables and fruit trees growing alongside artworks and repurposed objects, and each contains communal spaces intended to rejuvenate audiences while fostering dialogue about food access, empowerment, and freedom.

Ron Finley's *Grounded* features contributions from the following artists:

Cache
Jules Maskell and Eric Nicolas
Andrew McCarty
Wayne Perry
Pref
Ramsess

Pages 20–29:
Ron Finley, *Grounded*, 2024.
Installation view,
Hammer Museum,
Los Angeles, September 14,
2024–January 5, 2025.

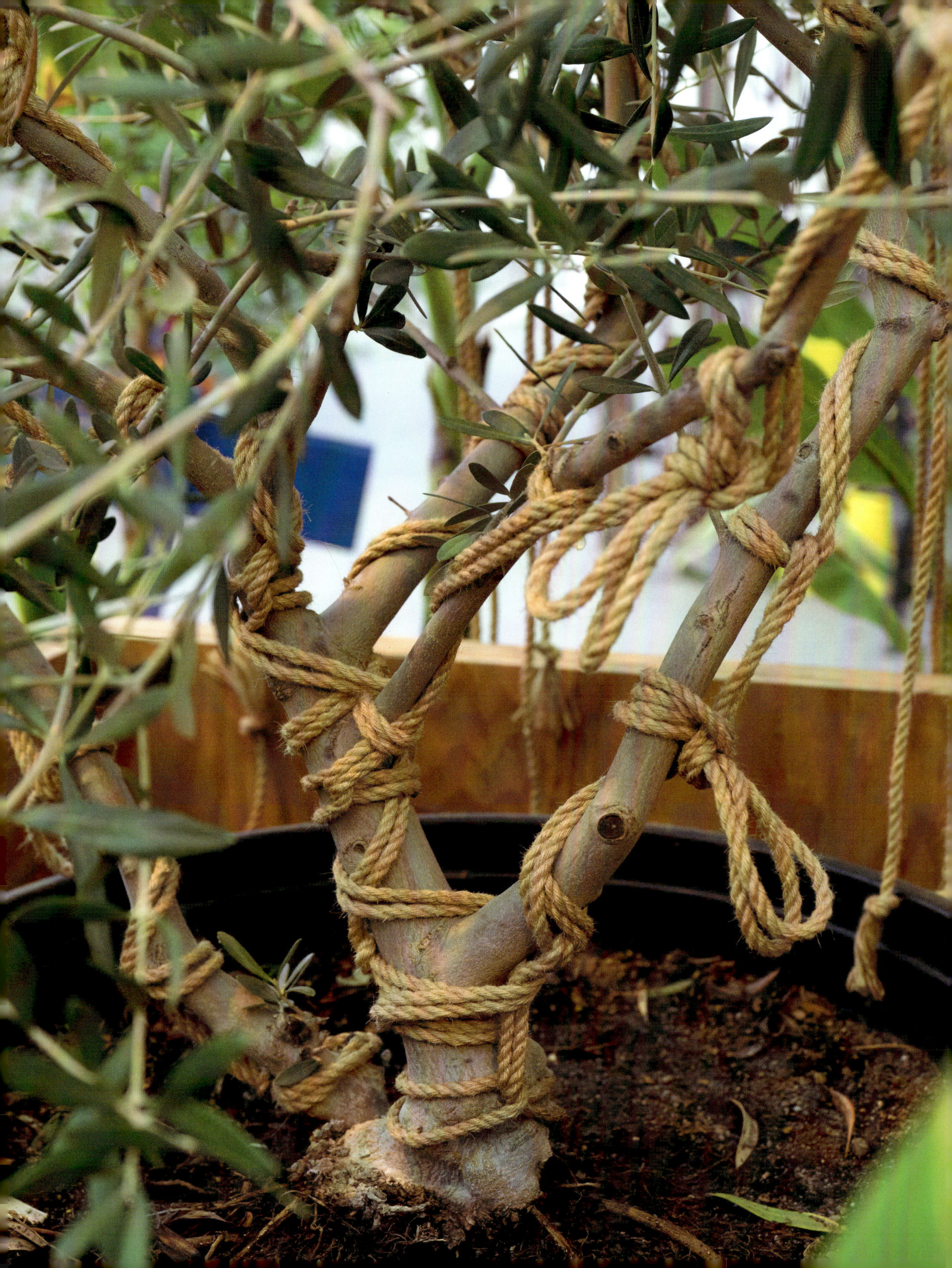

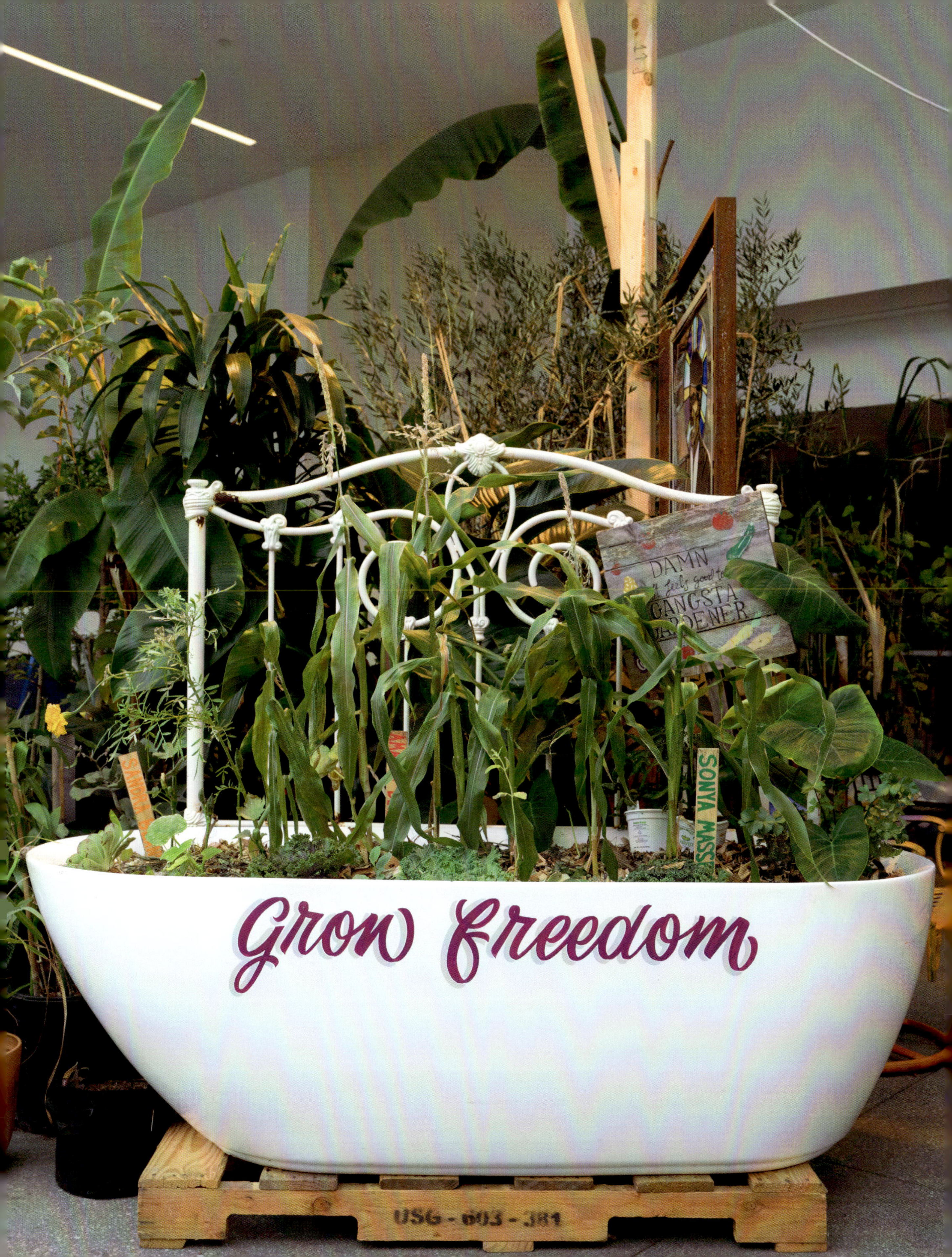
Grow Freedom
DAMN
it feels good to
GANGSTA
GARDENER
USG - 603 - 381

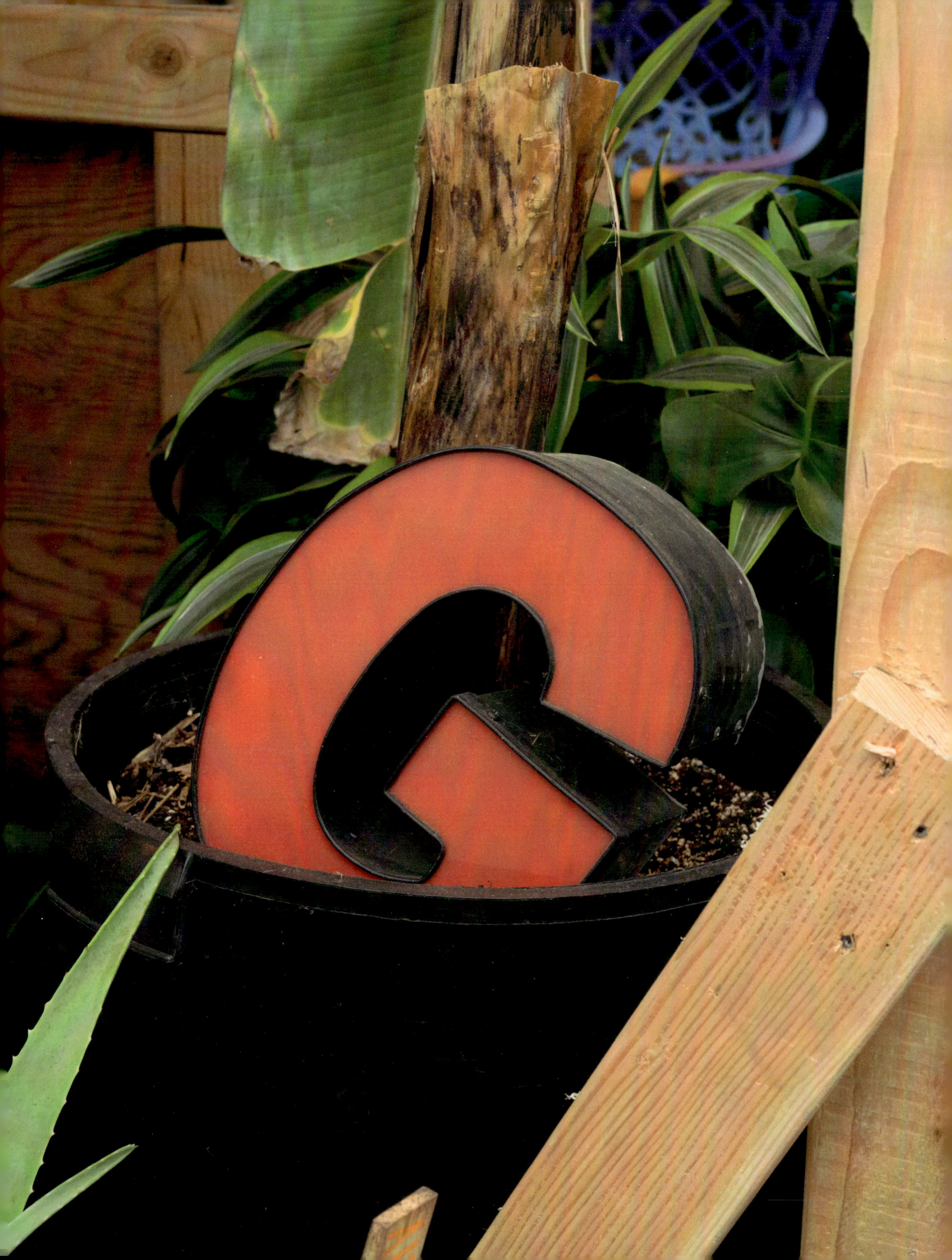

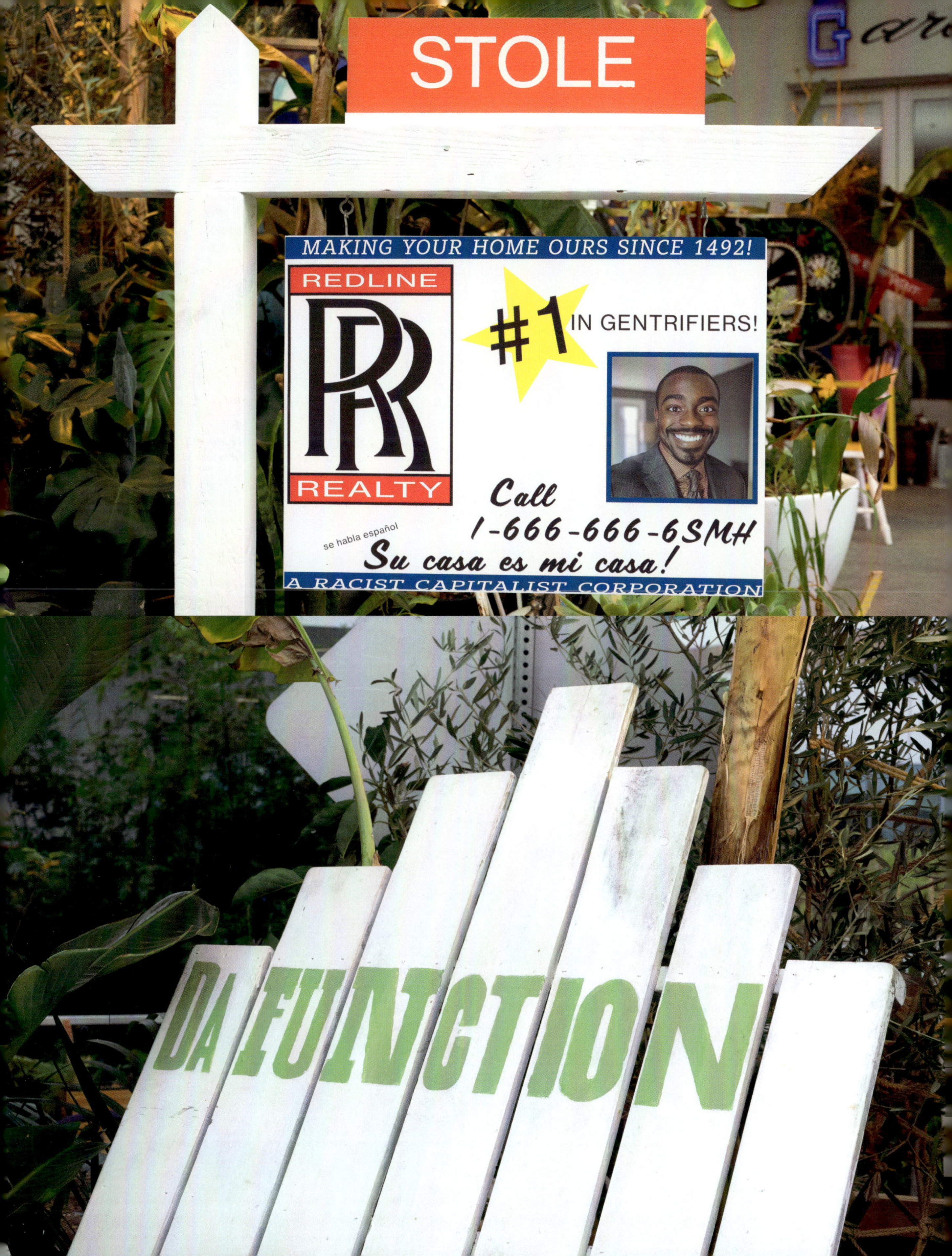
STOLE
MAKING YOUR HOME OURS SINCE 1492!
REDLINE
RR
REALTY
se habla español
#1 IN GENTRIFIERS!
Call
1-666-666-6SMH
Su casa es mi casa!
A RACIST CAPITALIST CORPORATION
DA FUNCTION

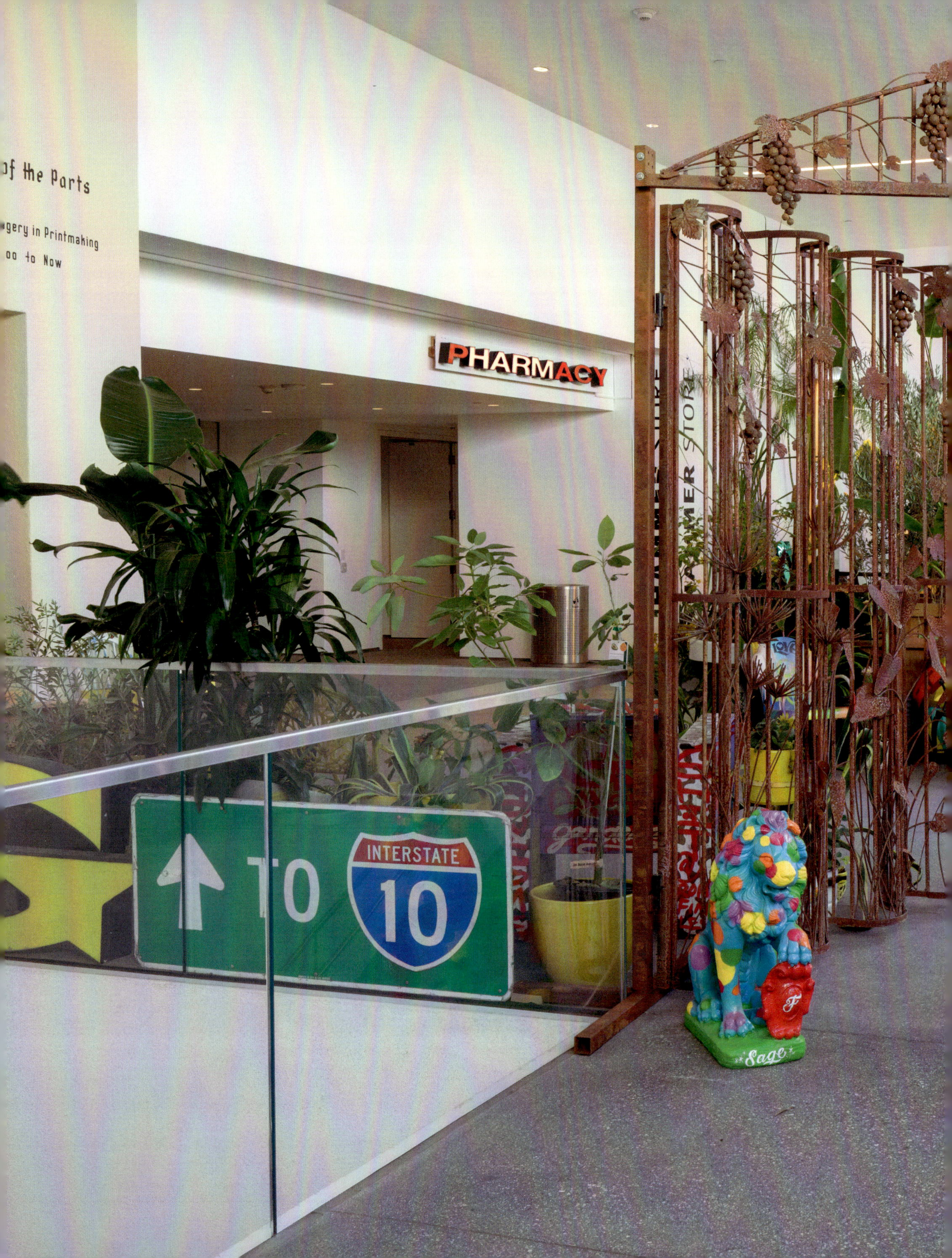
of the parts
gery in Printmaking
oo to Now
PHARMACY
TO INTERSTATE 10
Sage

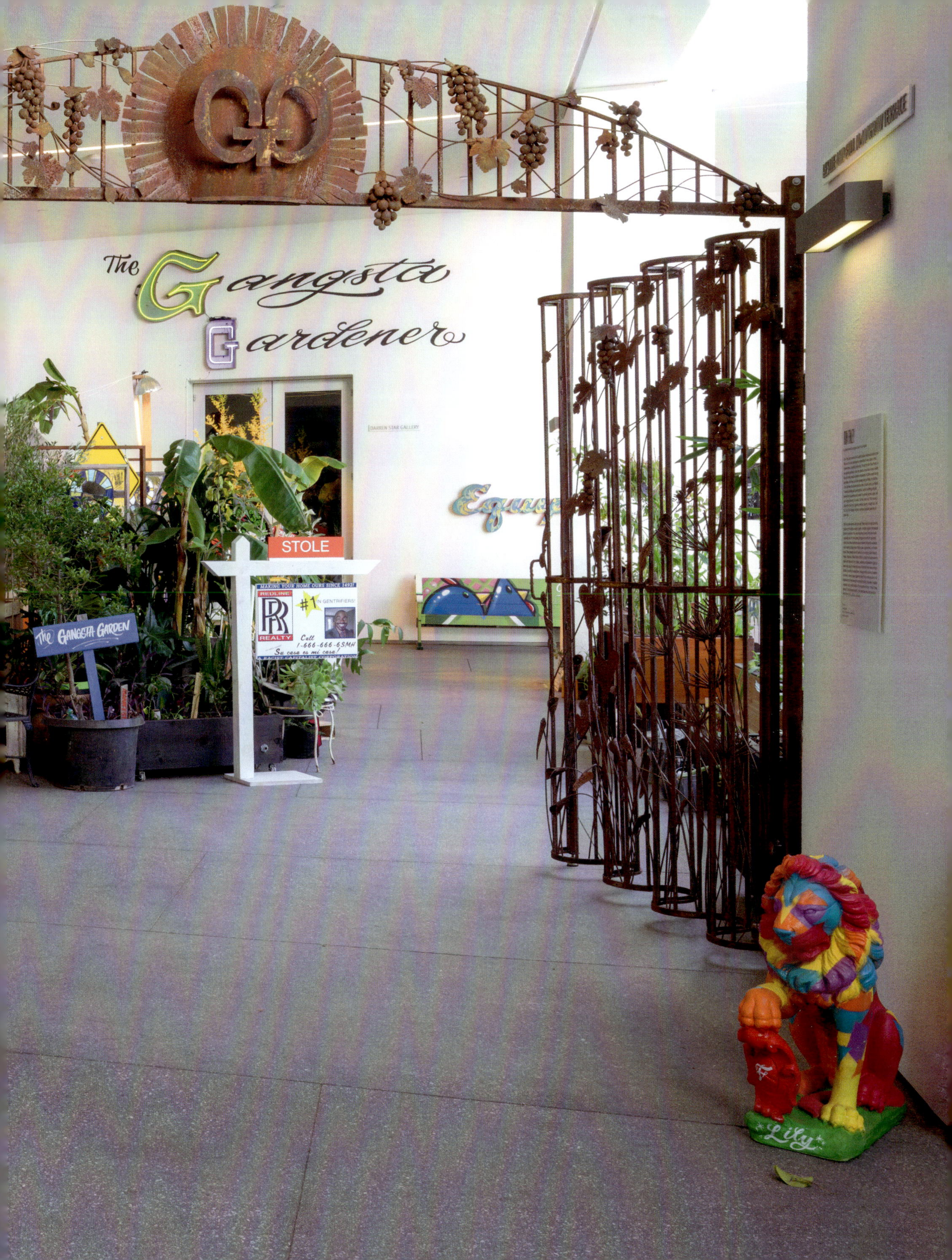

The Gangsta Gardener
DARREN STAR GALLERY
STOLE
MAKING YOUR HOME OURS SINCE 1492!
REDLINE
RR
REALTY
#1 IN GENTRIFIERS!
Call
1-666-666-6SMH
Su casa es mi casa!
A RACIST CAPITALIST CORPORATION
The Gangsta Garden
Equity
Lily

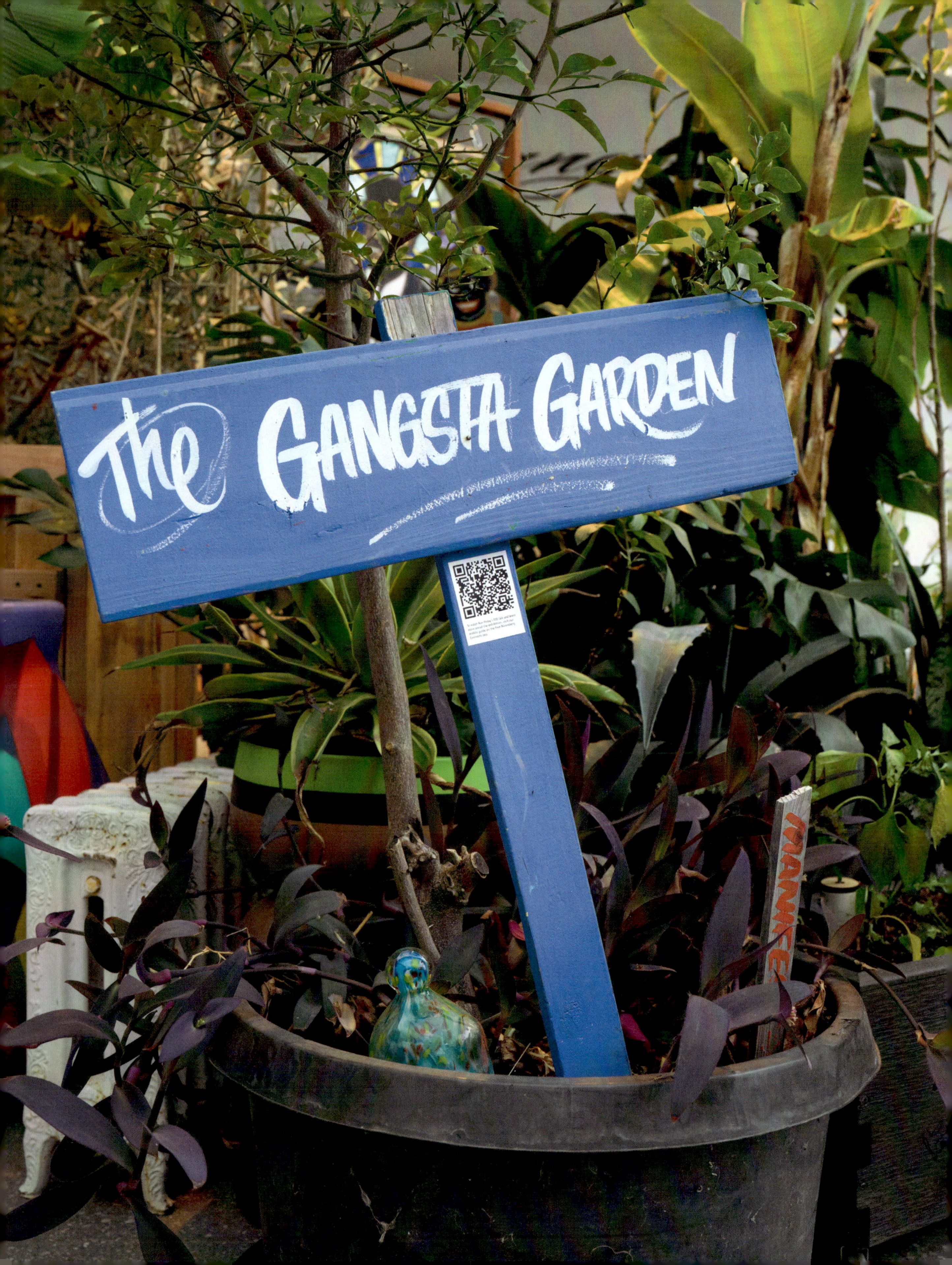
The Gangsta Garden

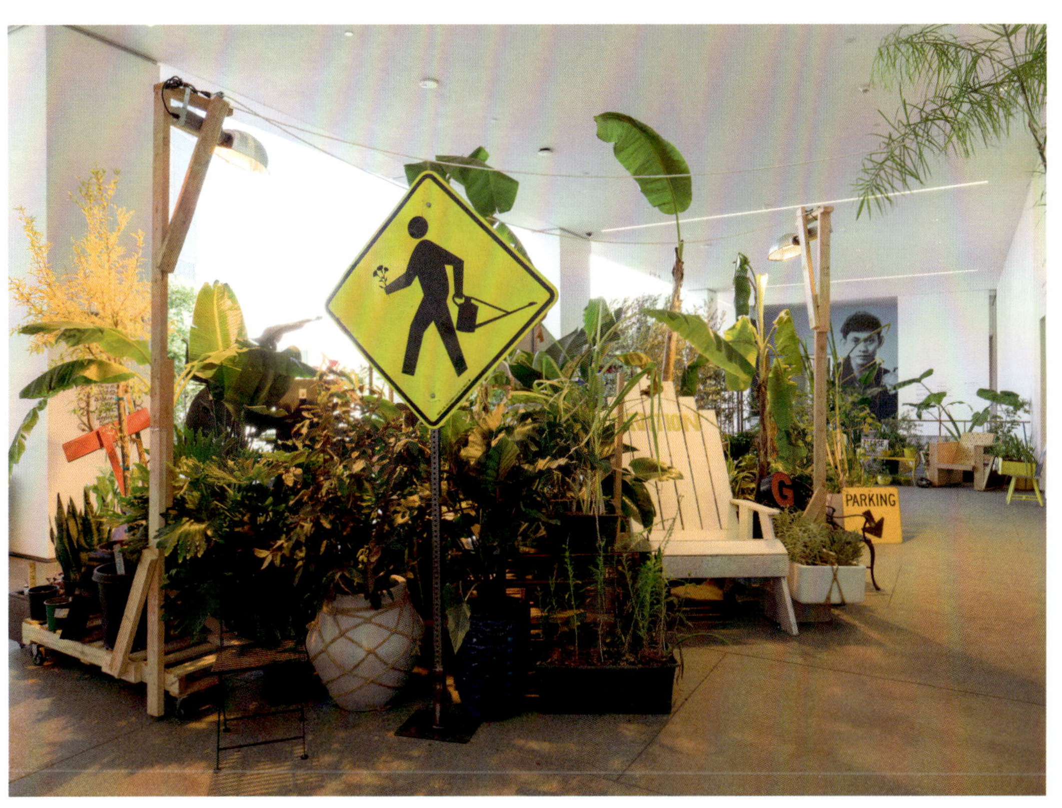

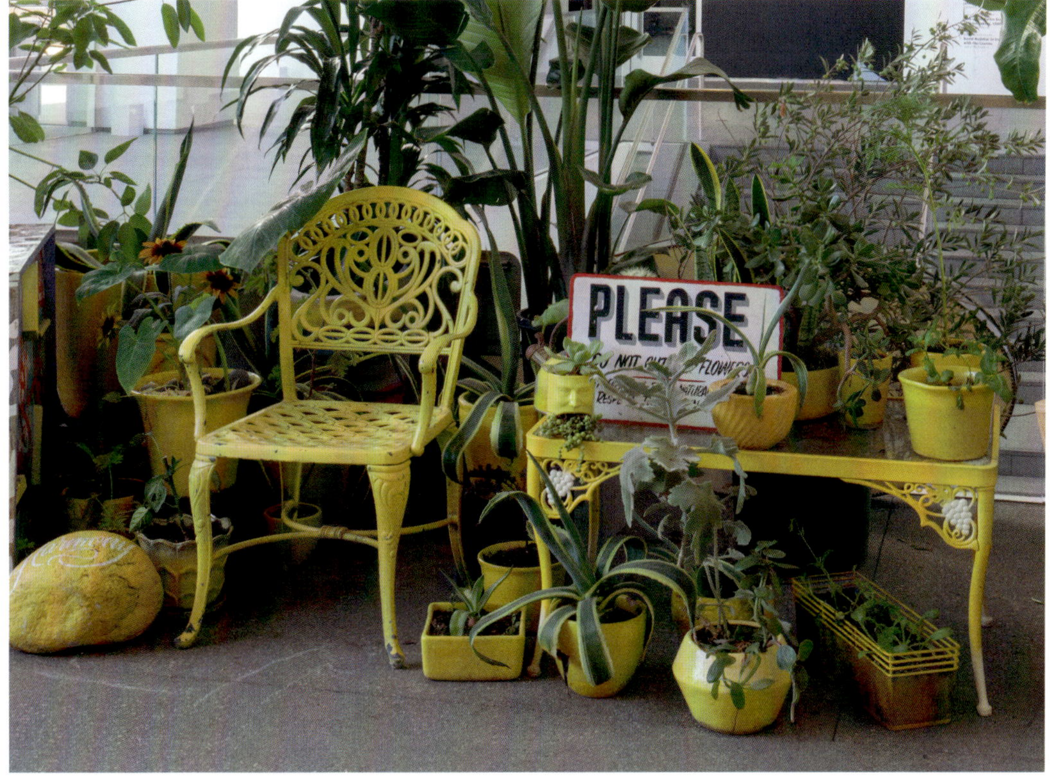

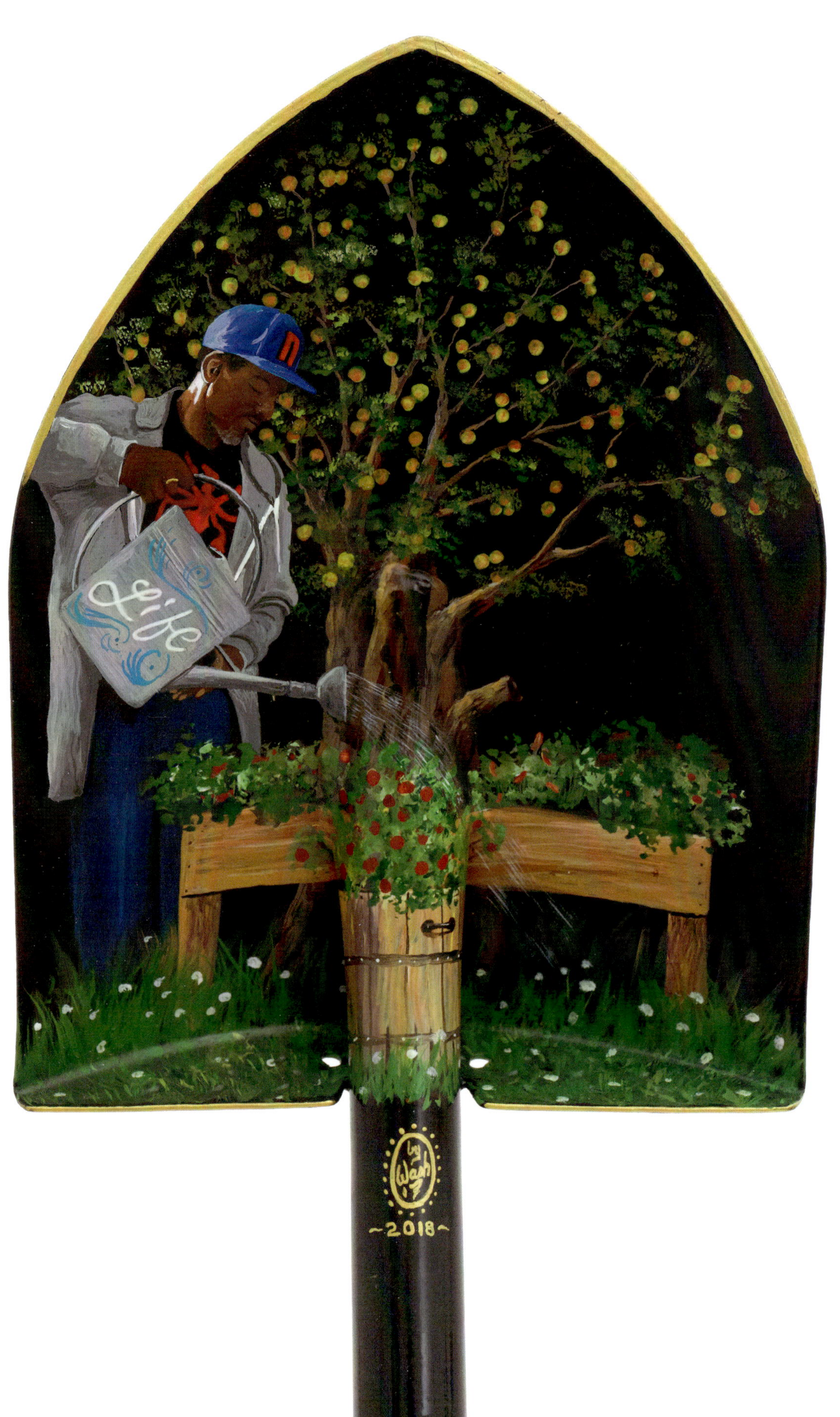

Life
by Wash
~2018~

URBAN WEAPONRY PROJECT, WEAPONS OF MASS CREATION (2018–)

Urban Weaponry Project, Weapons of Mass Creation (2018–) is a project that underscores Finley's deep-rooted devotion to art, design, gardening, and grassroots organizing. Seven years ago, he noticed that many of his artist friends were working in isolation. In an effort to connect them, Finley began inviting each one to transform a common, mass-produced gardening shovel into a distinctive work of art. A testament to his strength in community building, the installation at the Hammer represents only a small fraction of his expansive collection. "A tool of mass creation," as he frequently calls it, the shovel becomes a twin symbol of artistic production and food cultivation.

The installation as part of *Breath(e): Toward Climate and Social Justice* features contributions from the following artists:

Leigh Adams	Ron Finley	John Park
Aiseborn	Elizabeth Freitas	PAZ Love Crew
Lyndon Barrois, Sr.	Gajin Fujita	Lilia Ramirez aka Liliflor
Rodino Bautista	Sanae Guerin	Kam Redlawsk
Breonna and Farley Bliss	Andrew Hem	Adele Renault
Chaz Bojórquez	Alex Kizu aka DEFER	Rafael Reyes
Clinton Bopp	Augustine Kofie	Jose "Prime" Reza
Milton Bowens	Grace Lynne	Manny Sayes
Daphne Burgess	Patrick Martinez	Robert Standish
Chris Clayton	Karlos "BUMPS" Marquez	Hank Willis Thomas
Greg "Craola" Simkins	Michael Massenburg	Shark Toof
Brett Crawford	Melissa Meier	Migz Miguel Torres
Charles Dickson	Patrice Moretti aka Smog One	Marc Trujillo
Ronald Feghali	Sean Norvet	Richard T. Walsh
Delfin Finley	Noni Olabisi	MR. WASH
Kohshin Finley	Mear One	Jaime "Germs" Zacarias

Page 30:
MR. WASH

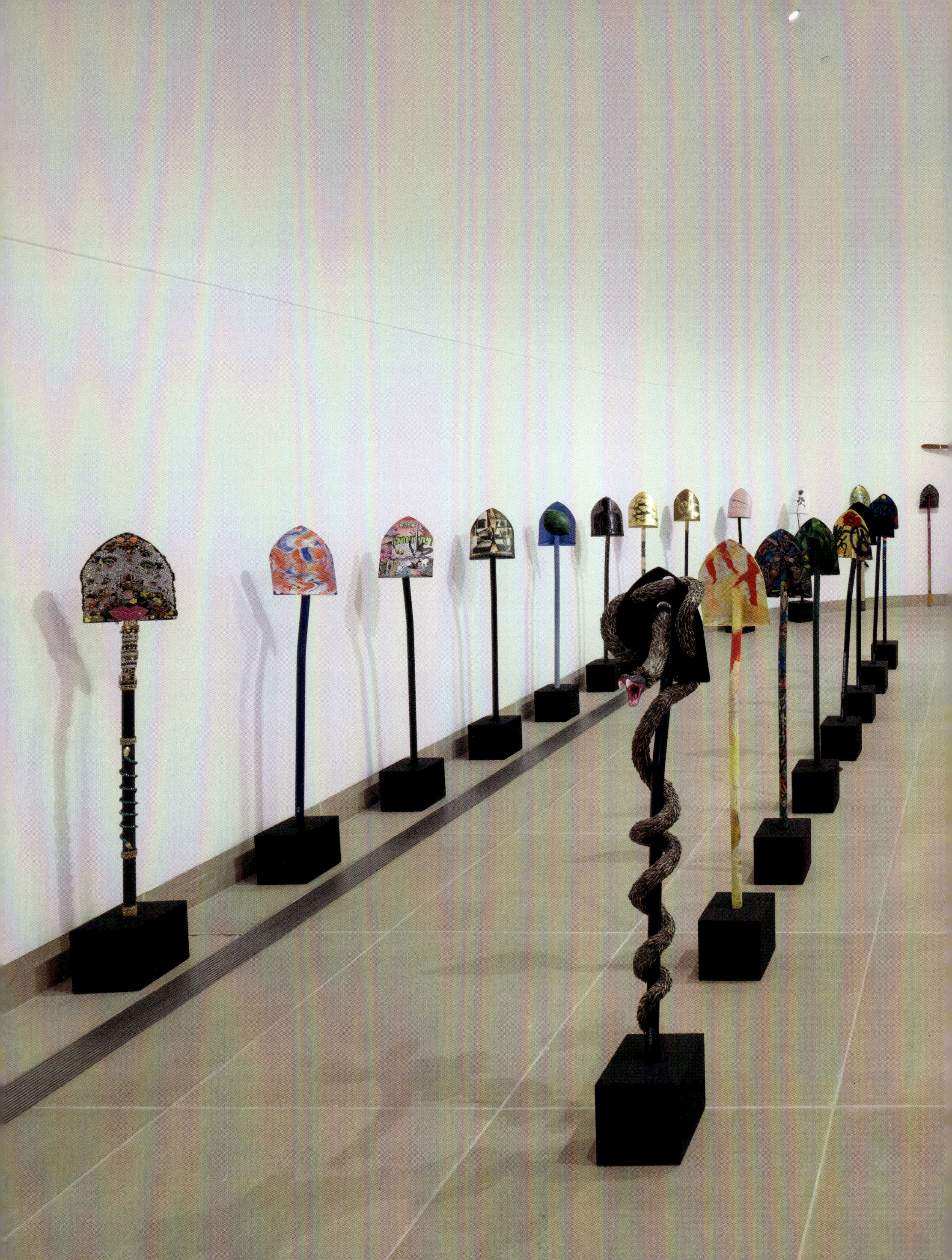

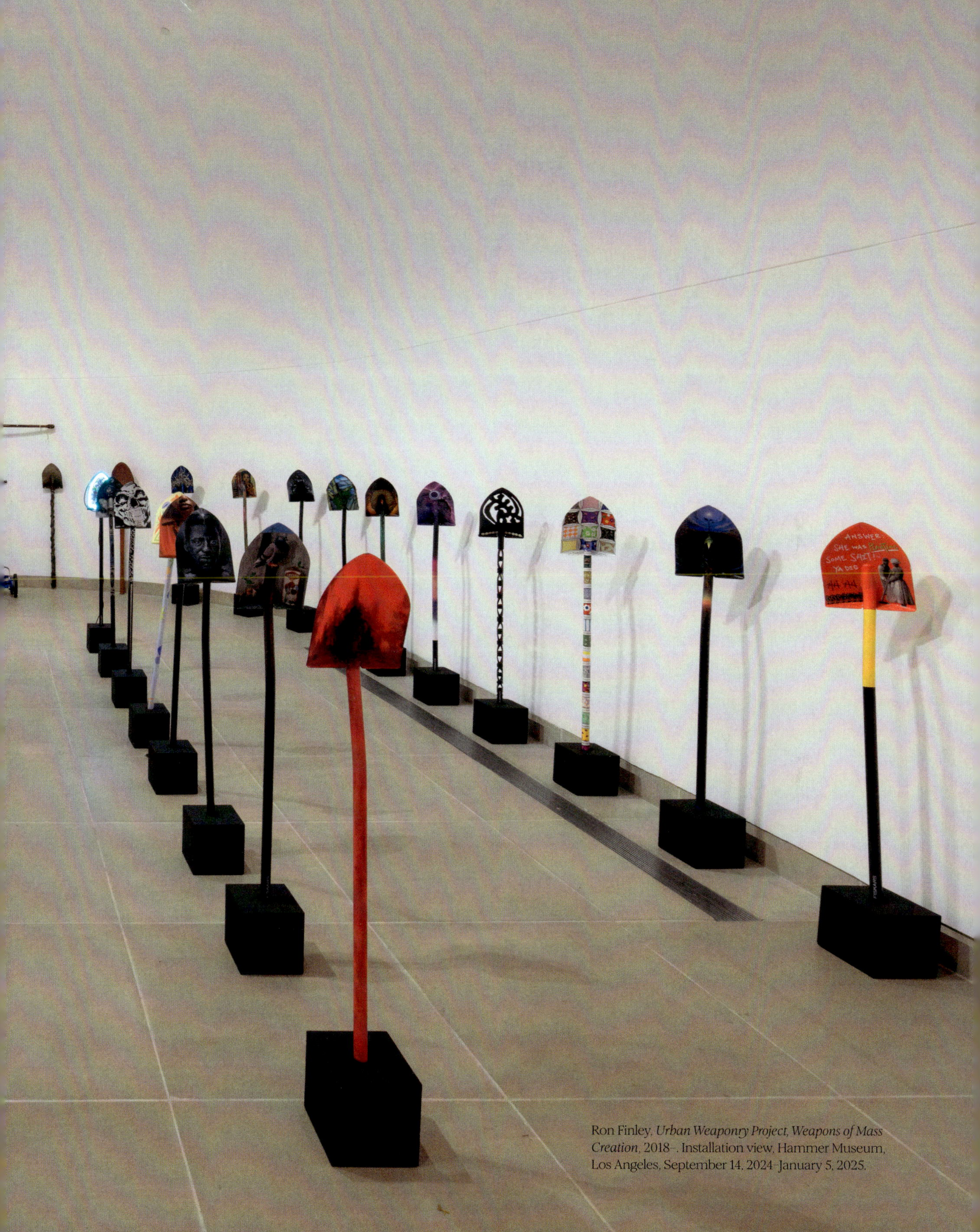

Ron Finley, *Urban Weaponry Project, Weapons of Mass Creation*, 2018–. Installation view, Hammer Museum, Los Angeles, September 14, 2024–January 5, 2025.

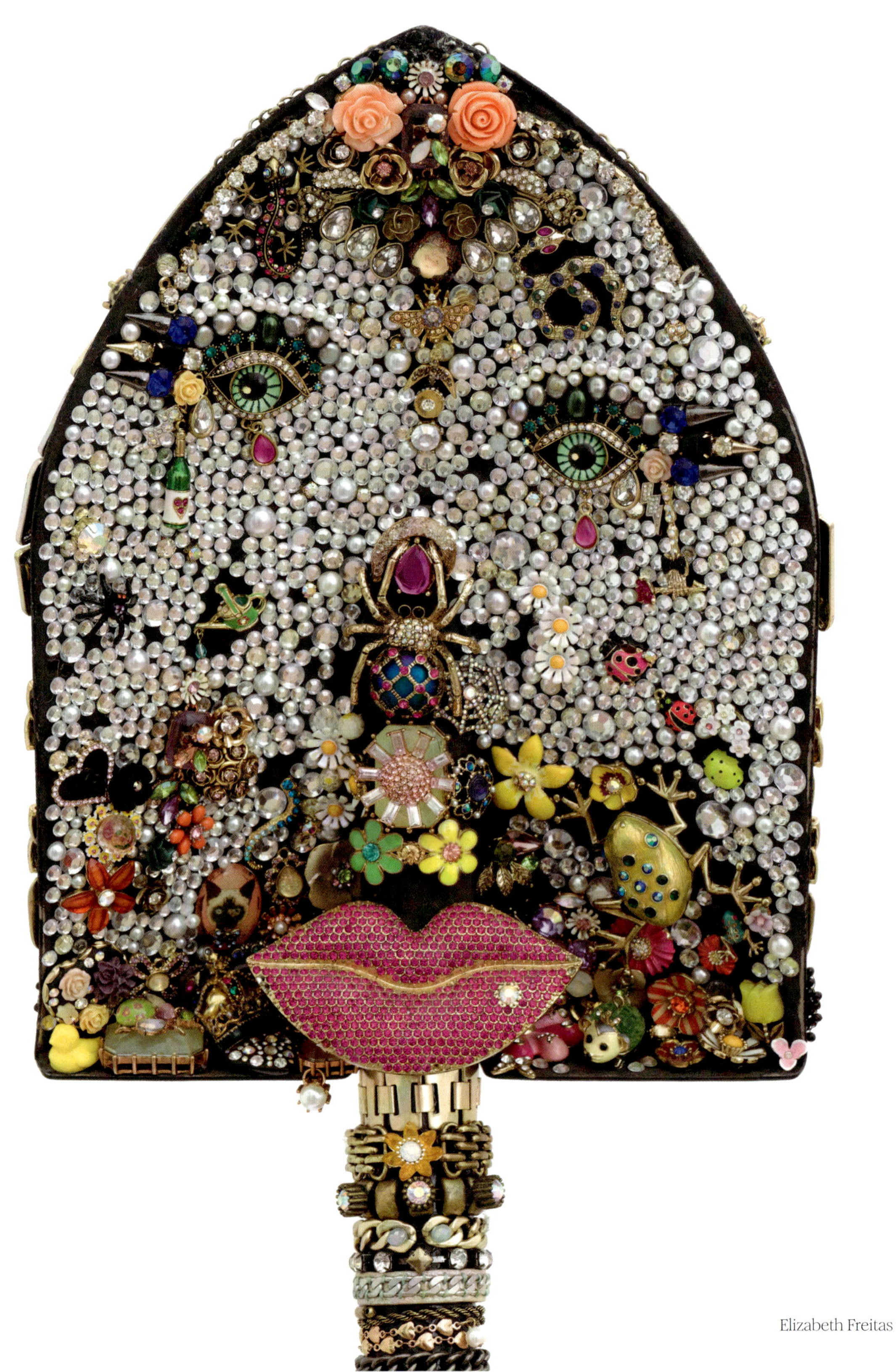

Elizabeth Freitas (front)

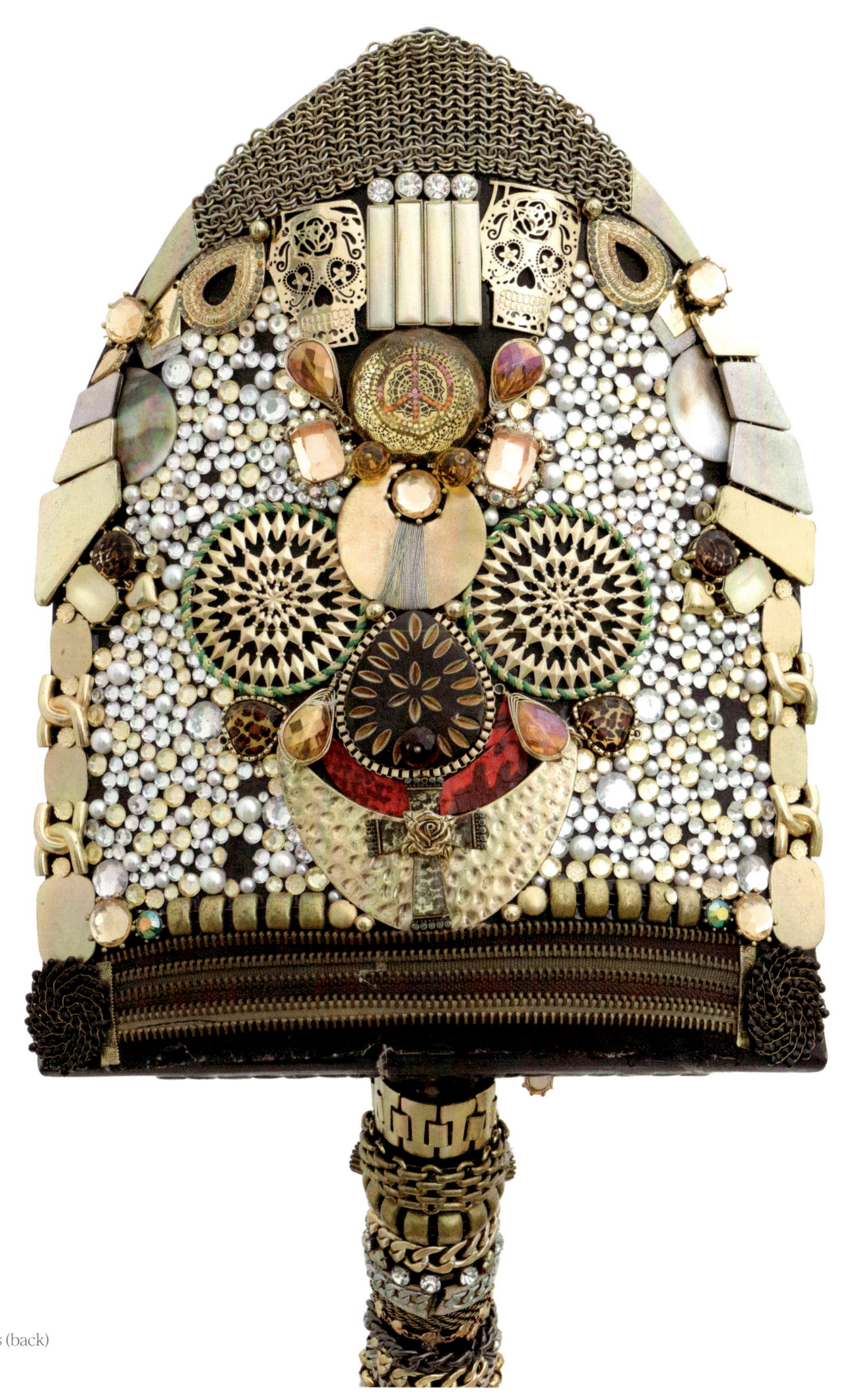

Elizabeth Freitas (back)

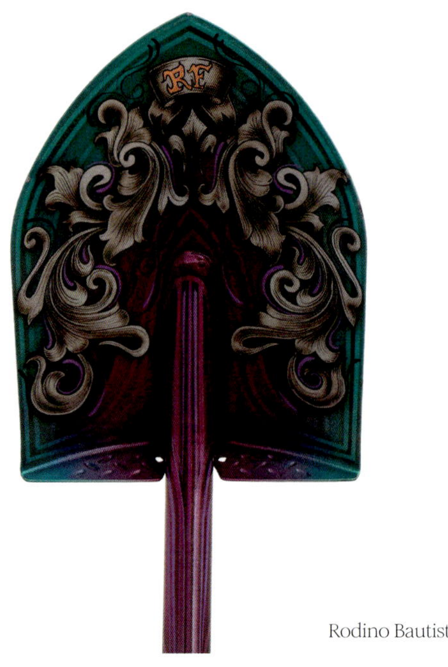

Rodino Bautista

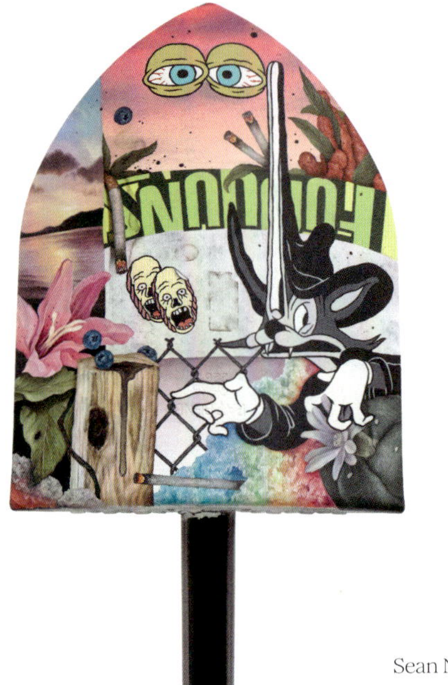

Sean Norvet

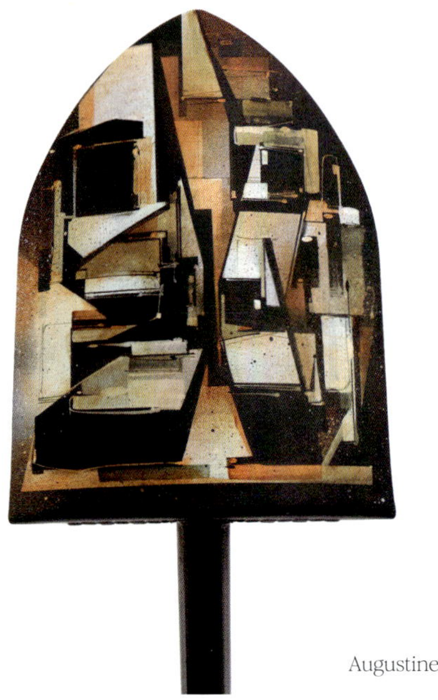

Augustine Kofie

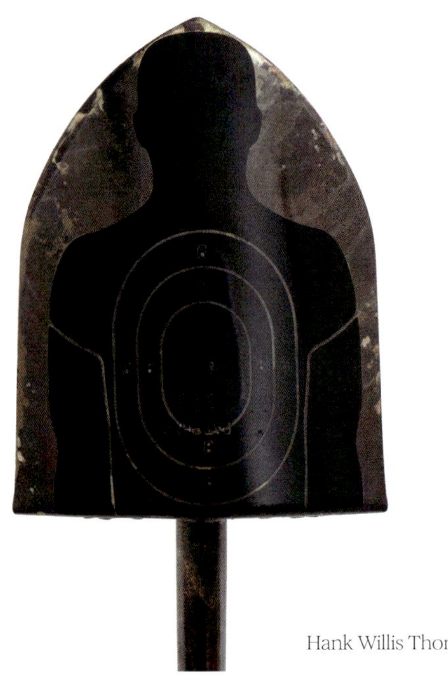

Hank Willis Thomas

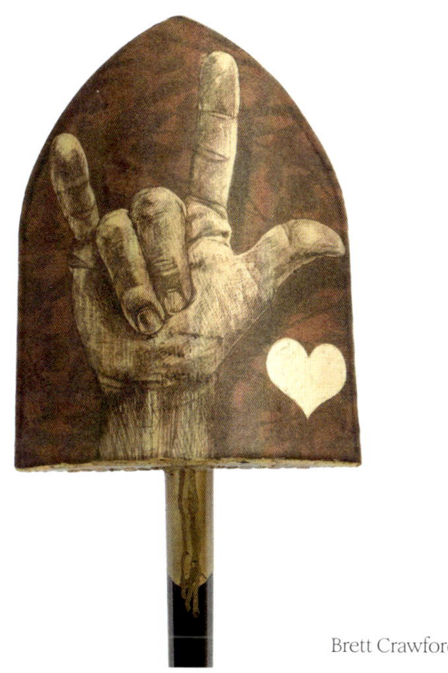

Brett Crawford

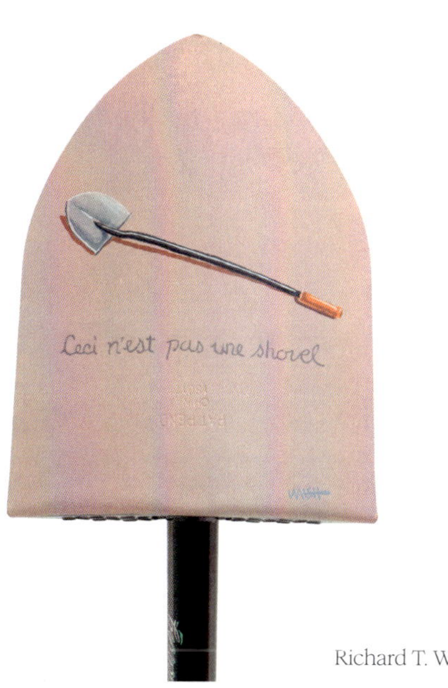

Richard T. Walsh

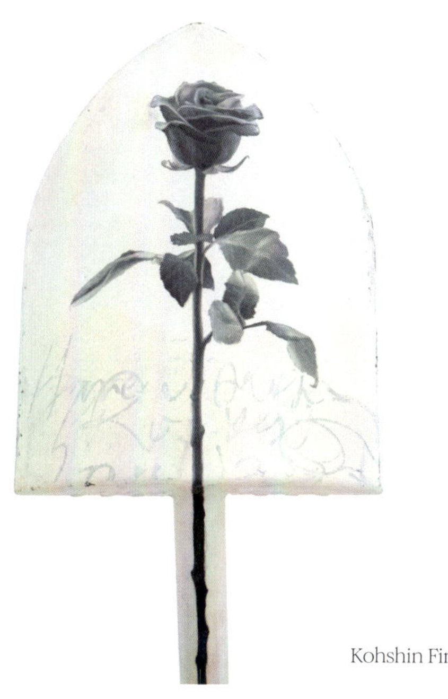

Kohshin Finley

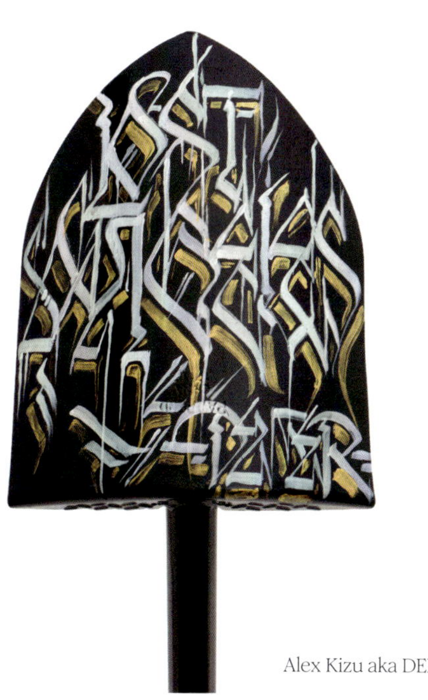

Alex Kizu aka DEFER

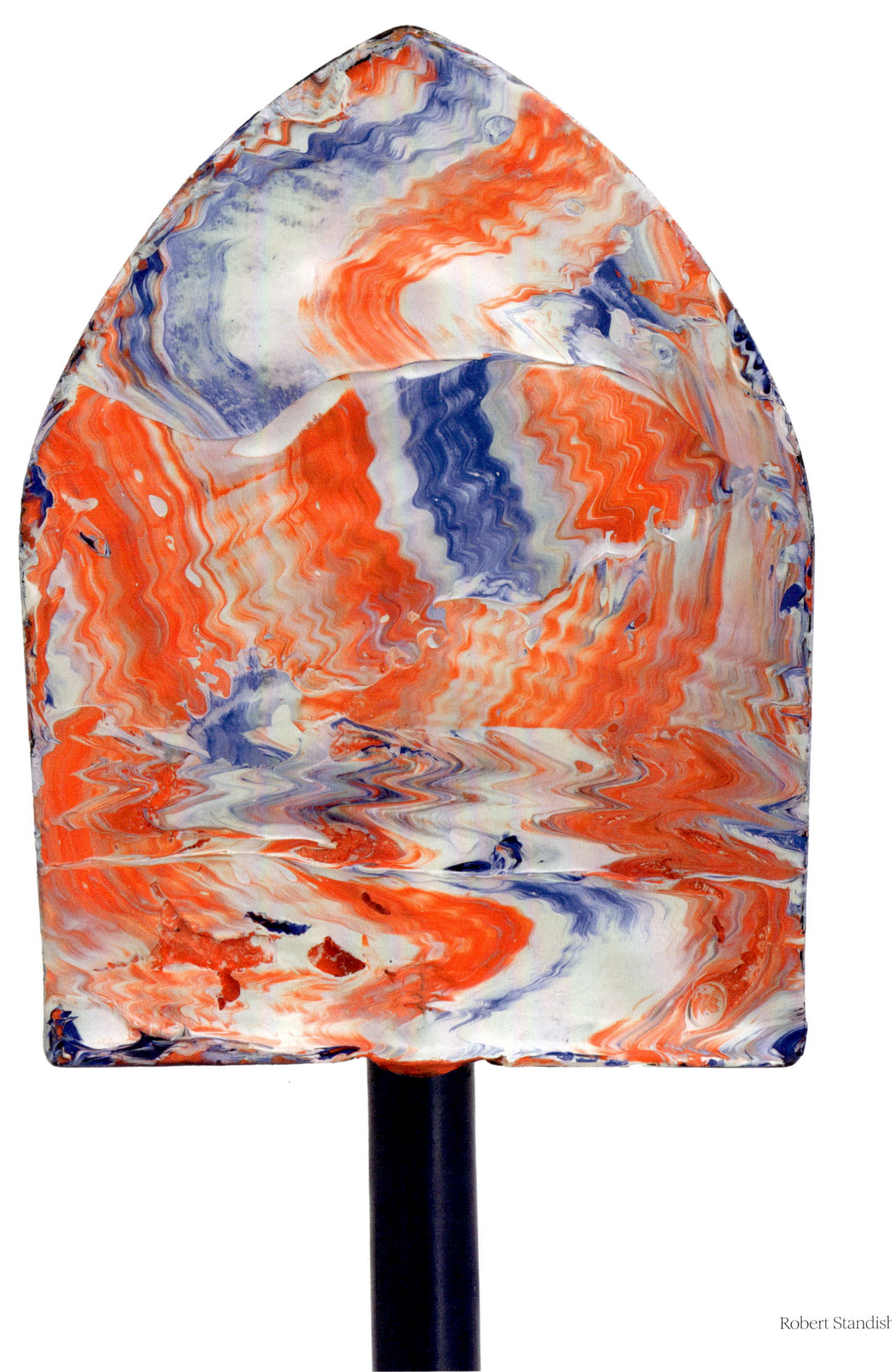

     RON FINLEY

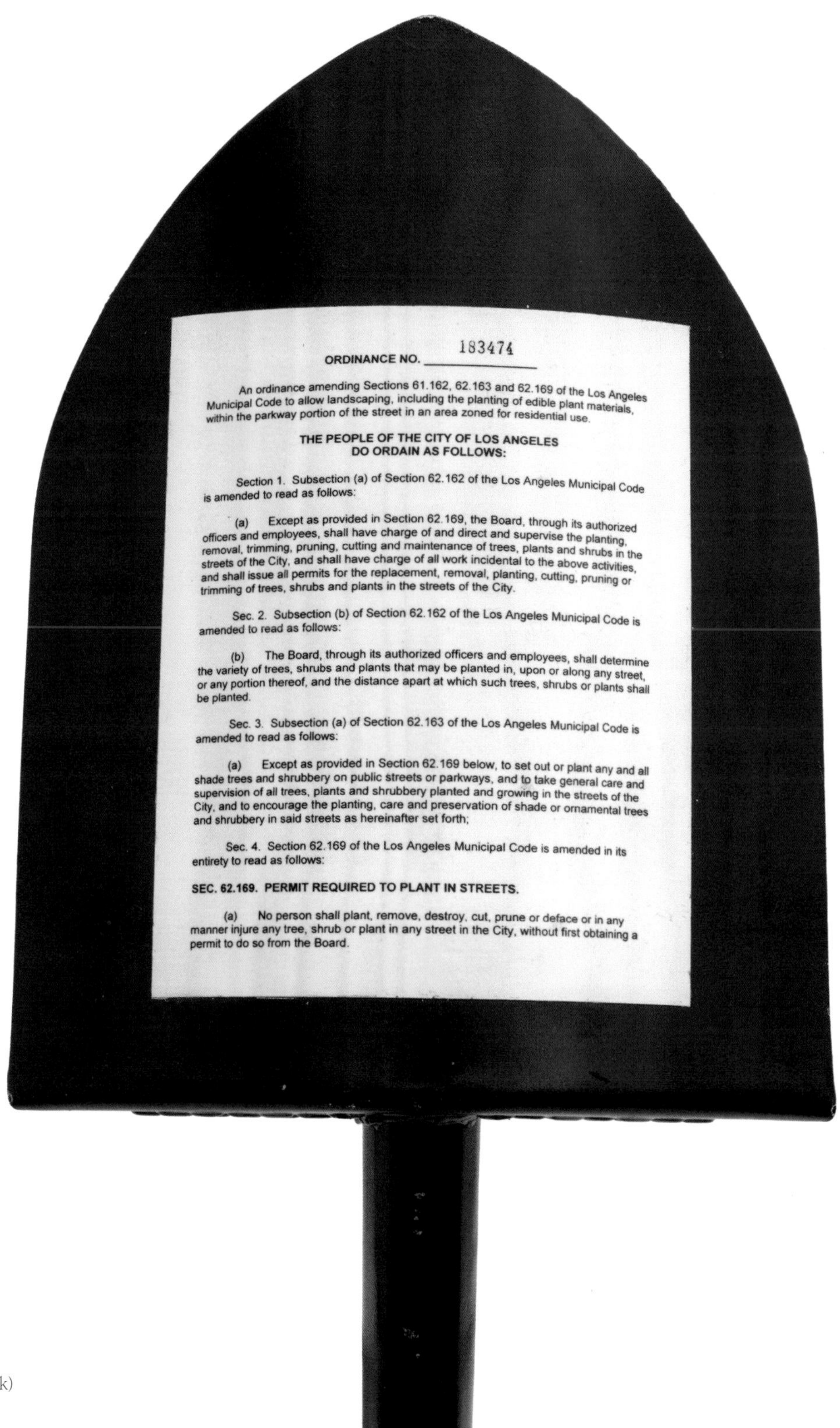

Robert Standish (back)

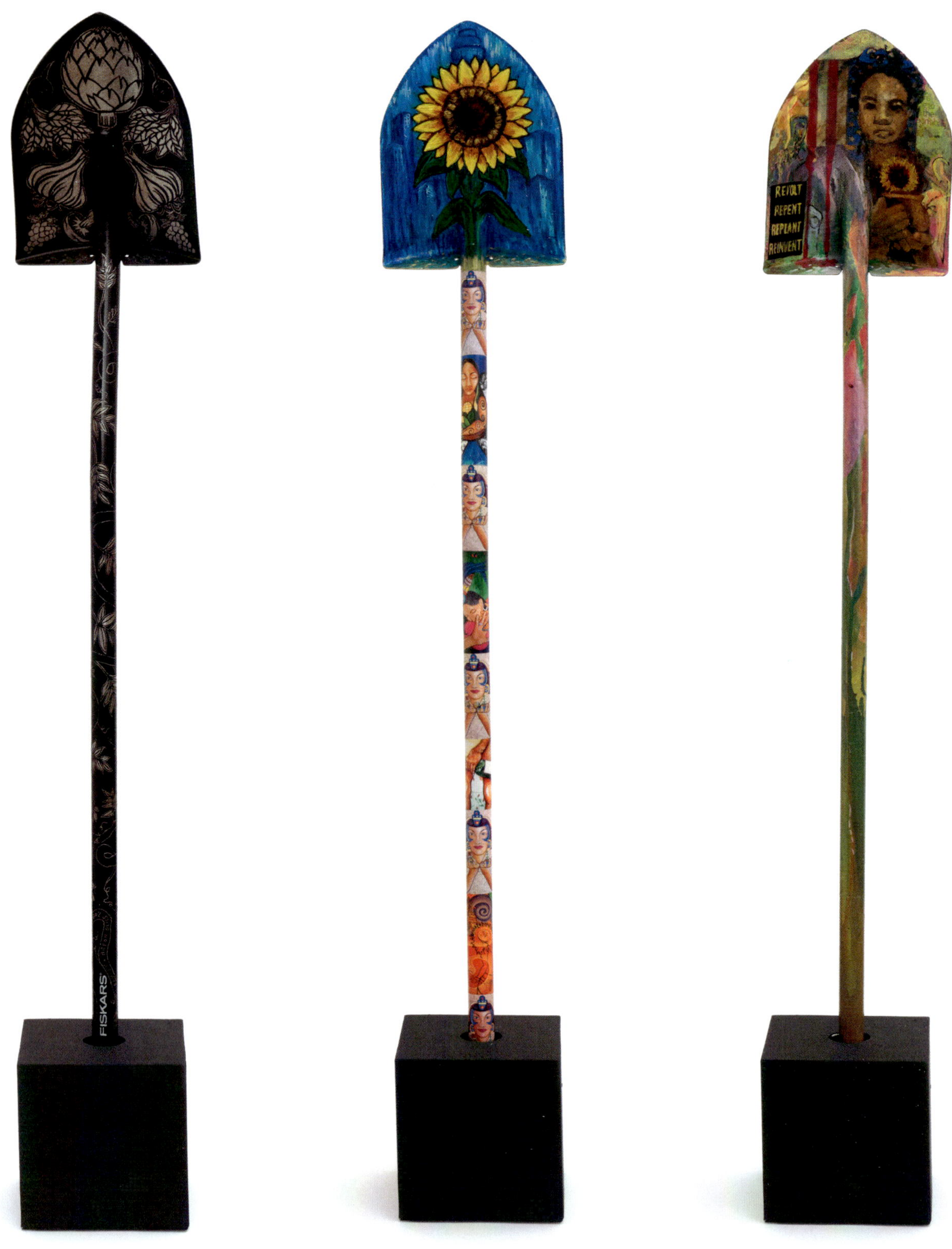

Breonna and Farley Bliss

Lilia Ramirez aka Liliflor

Michael Massenburg

 RON FINLEY

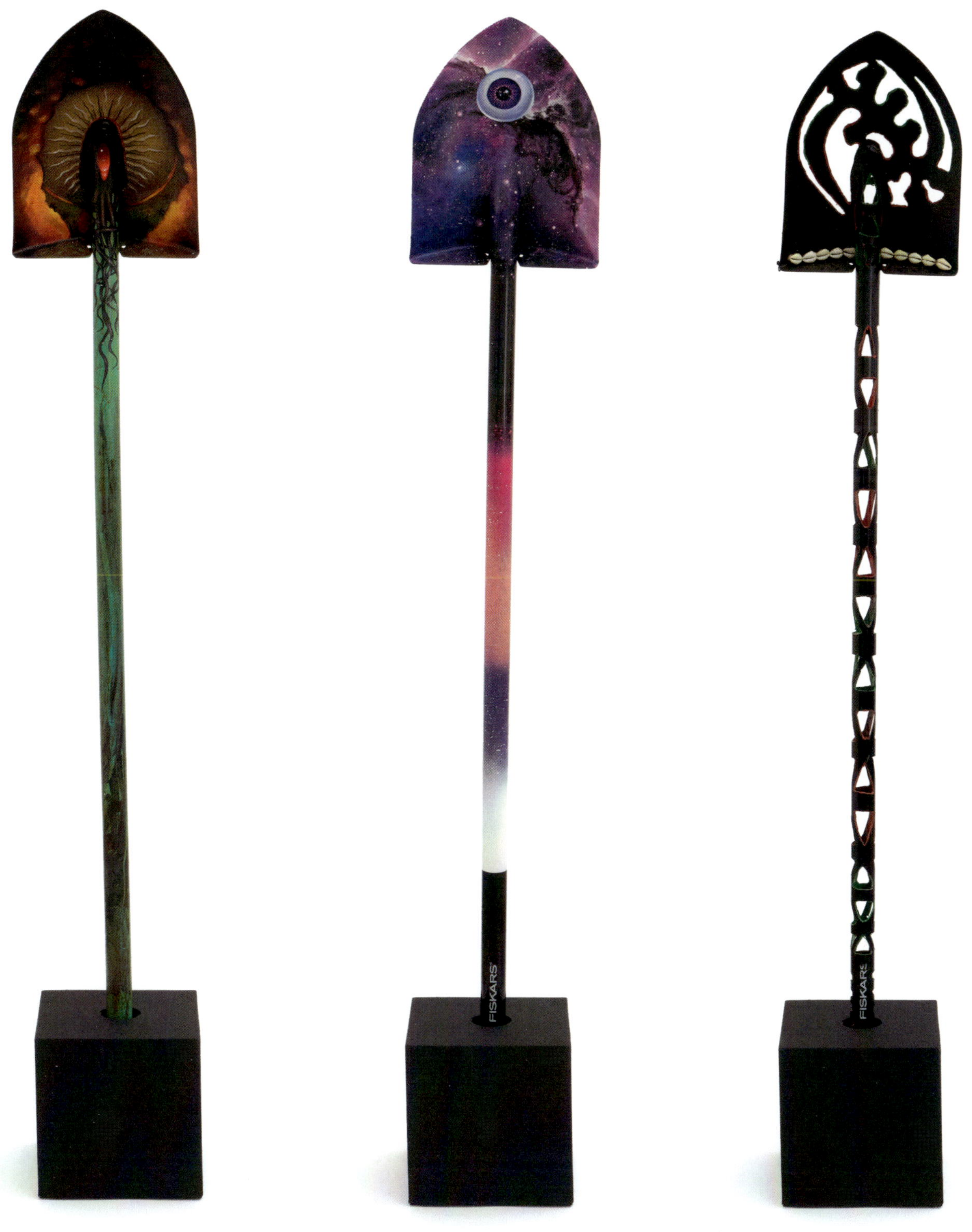

Jaime "Germs" Zacarias

Mear One

Charles Dickson

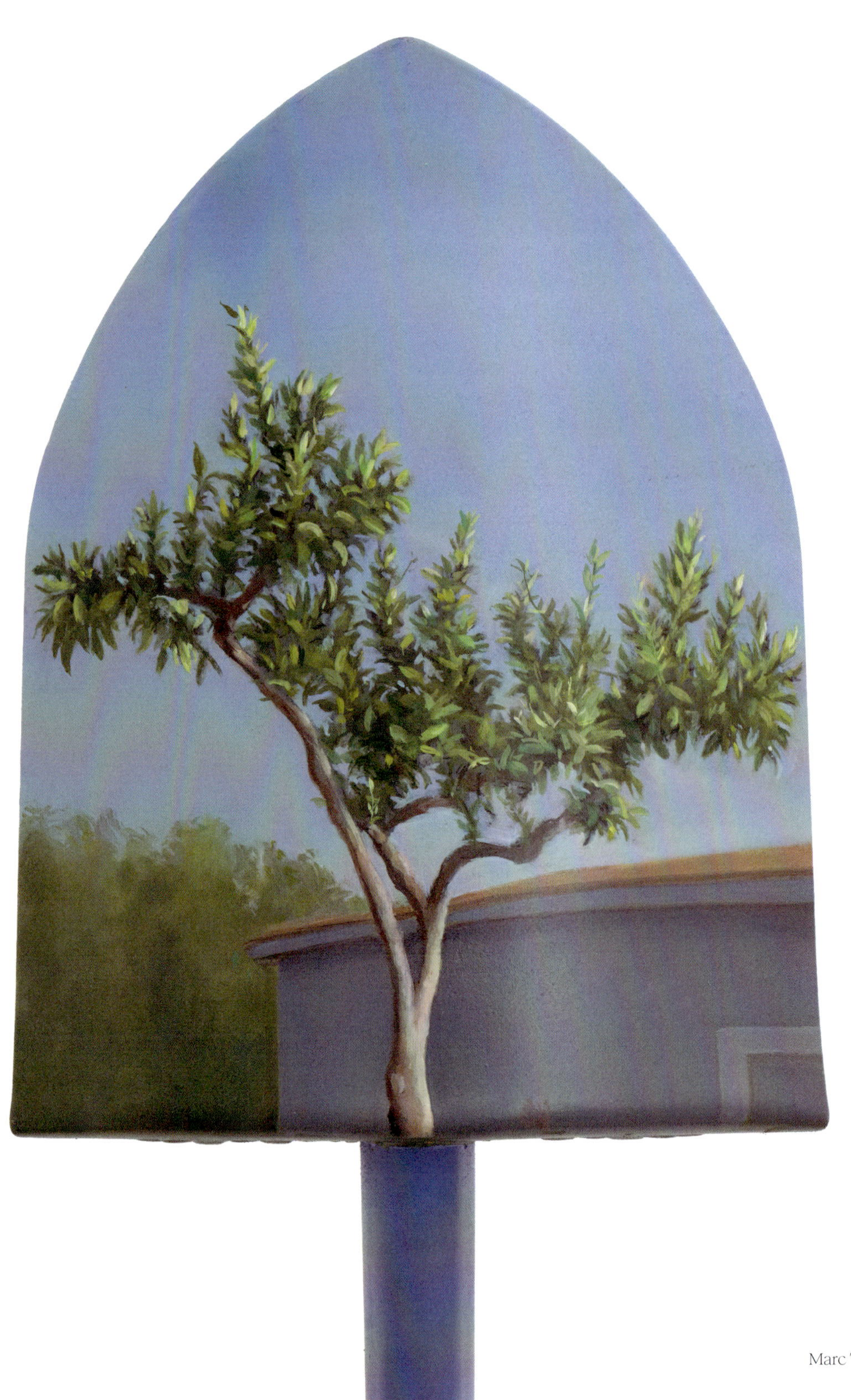

Marc Trujillo (back)

42   RON FINLEY

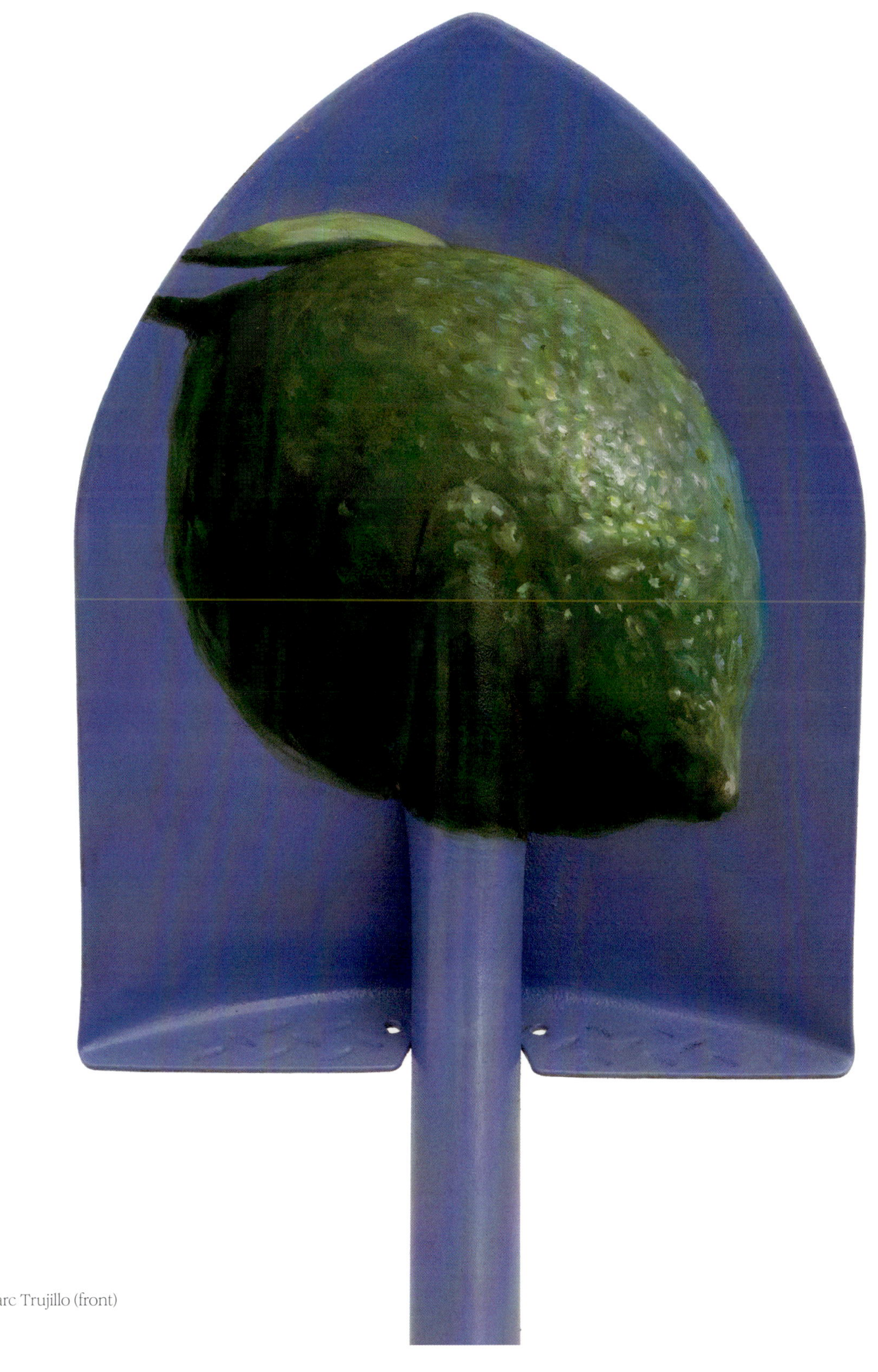

Marc Trujillo (front)

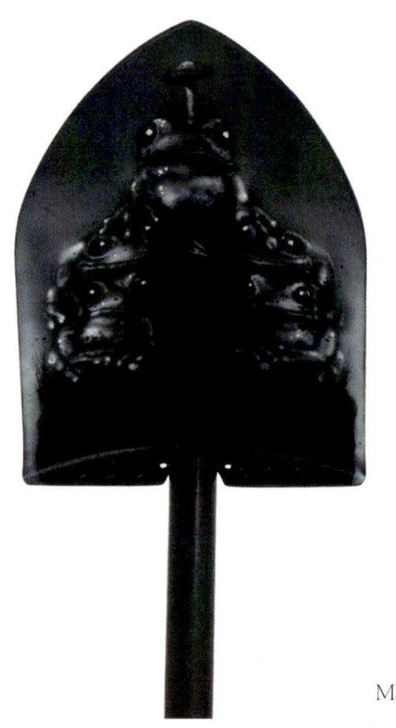

Manny Sayes

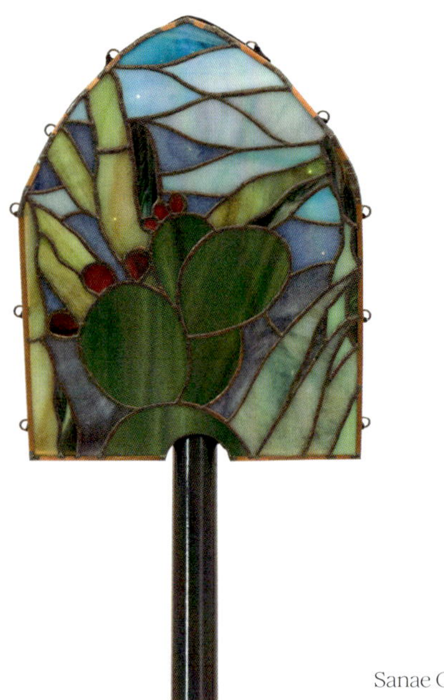

Sanae Guerin

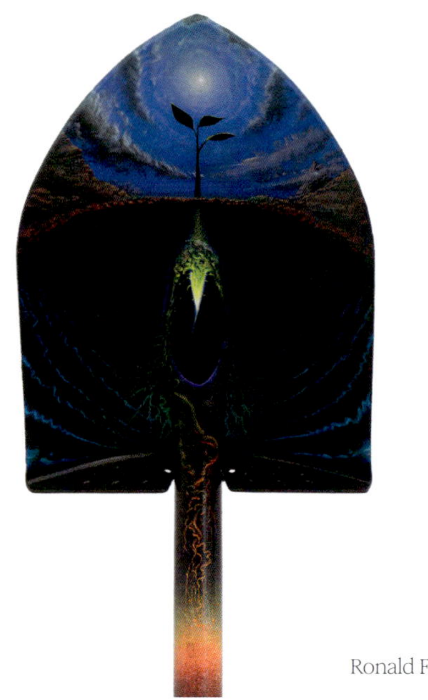

Ronald Feghali

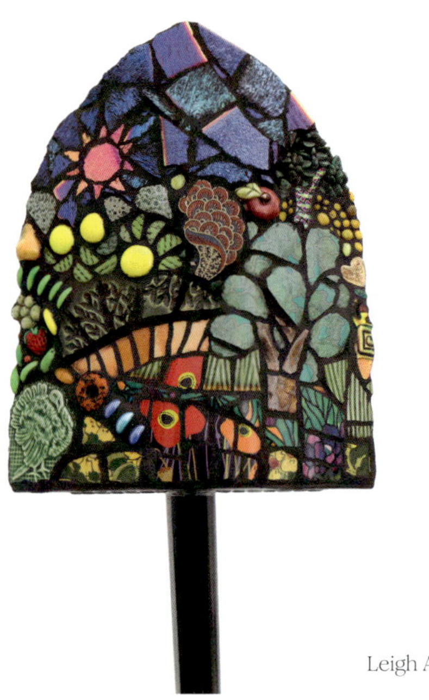

Leigh Adams

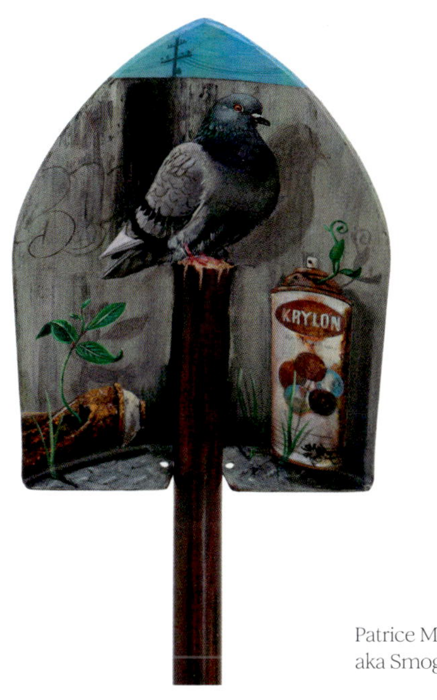

Patrice Moretti
aka Smog One

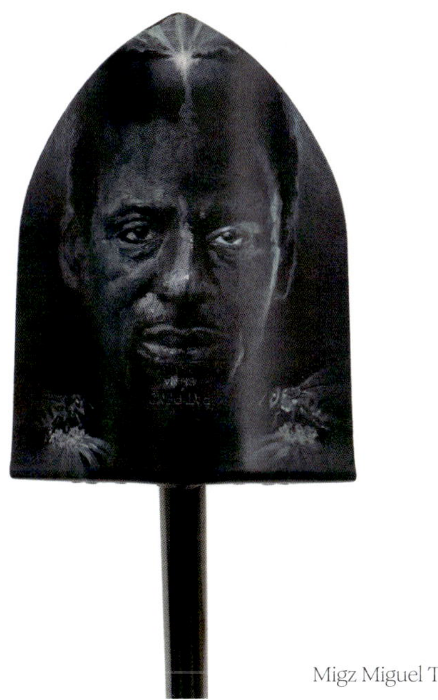

Migz Miguel Torres

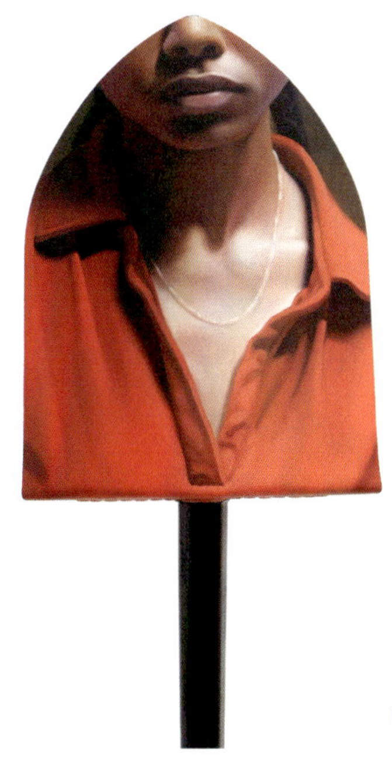

Delfin Finley

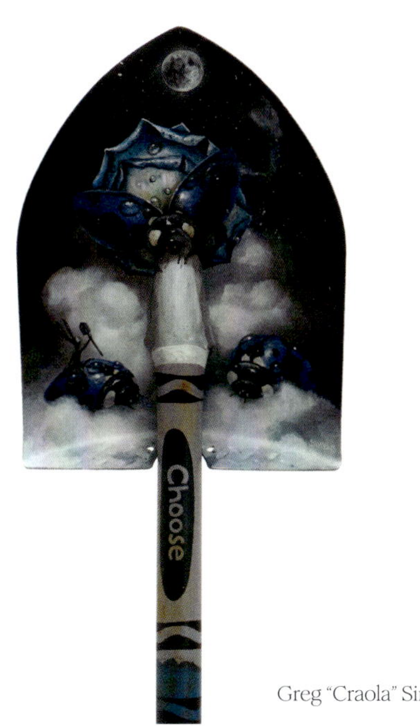

Greg "Craola" Simkins

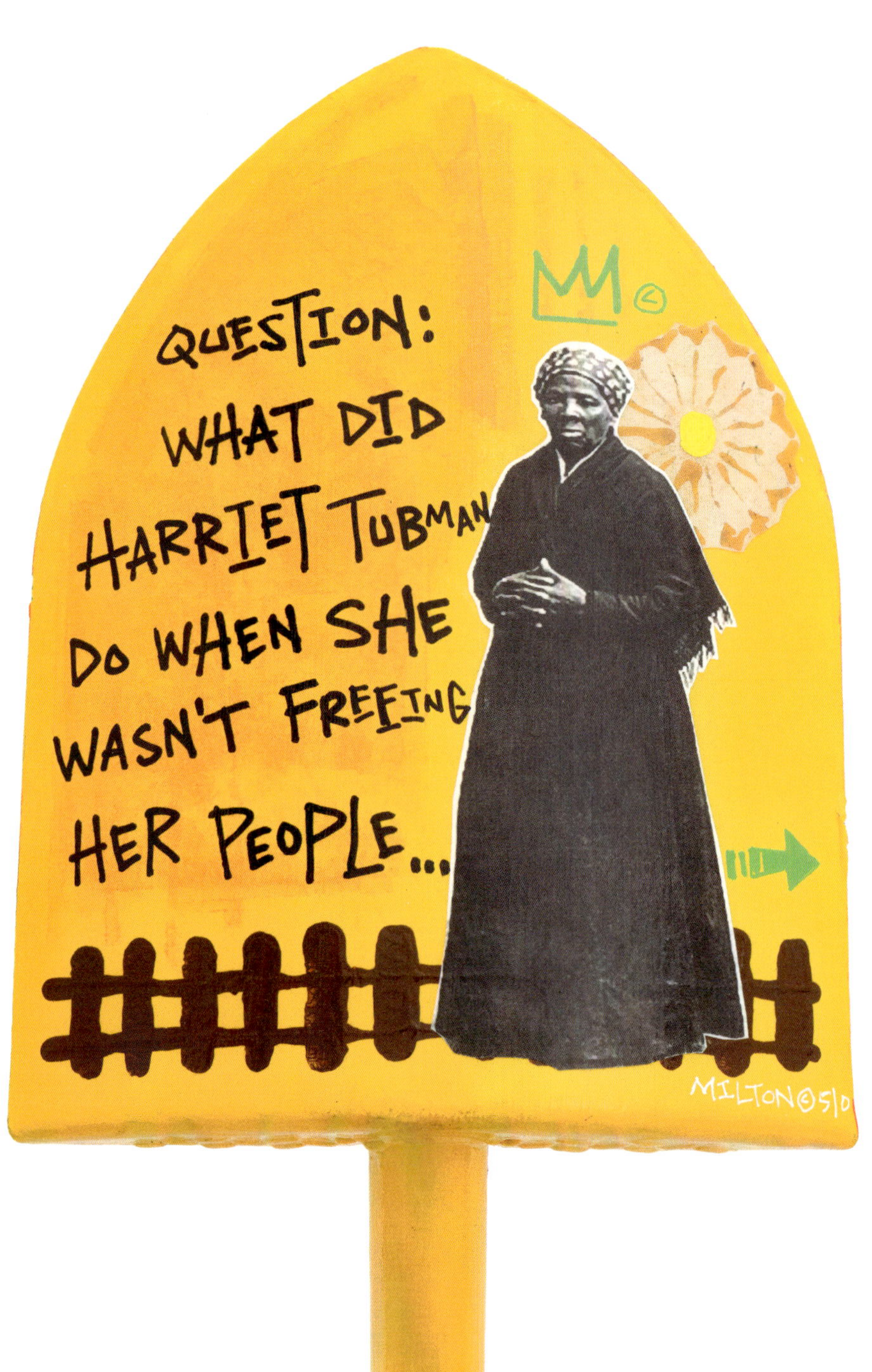

Milton Bowens (back)

     RON FINLEY

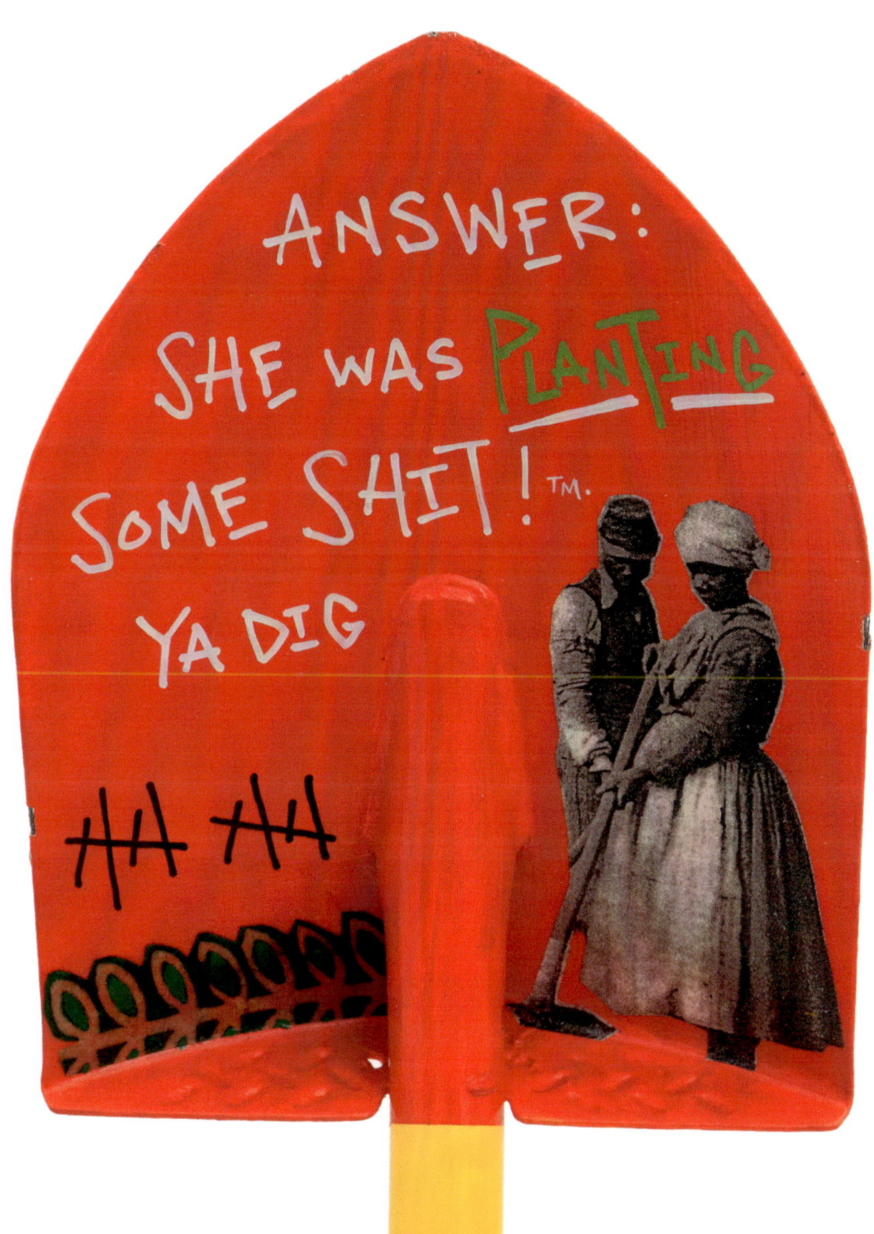

Milton Bowens (front)

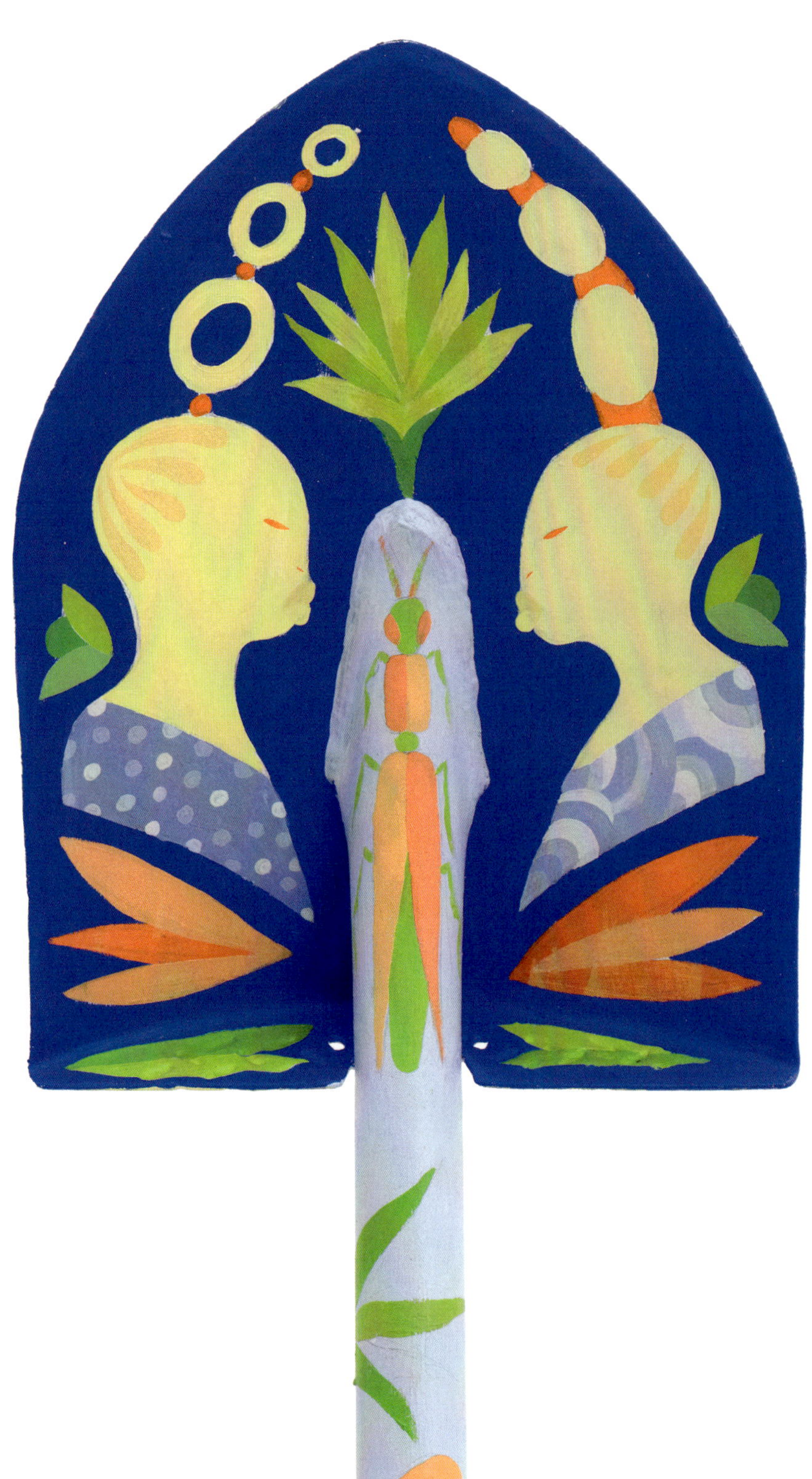

Grace Lynne (front)

   RON FINLEY

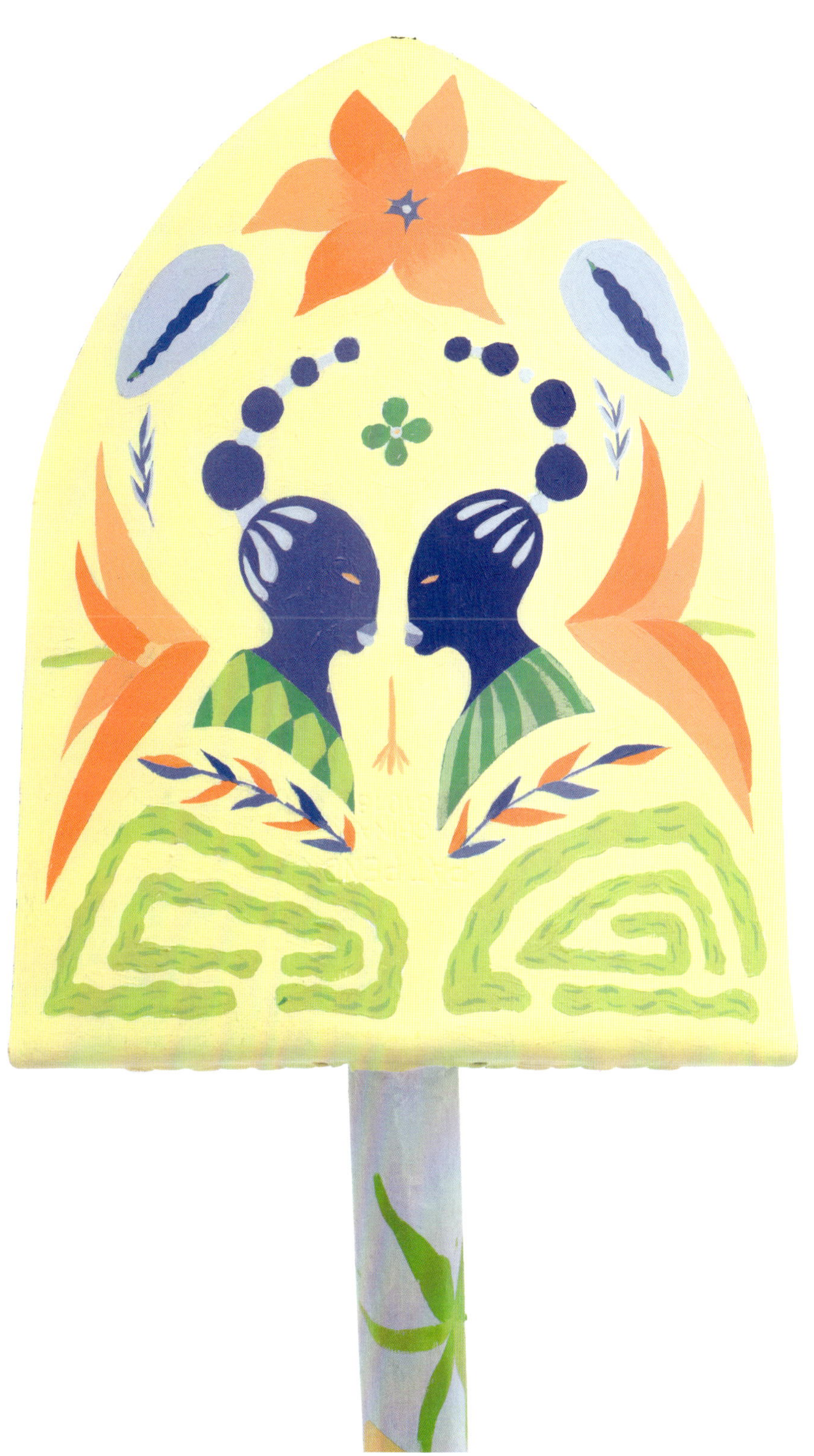

Grace Lynne (back)

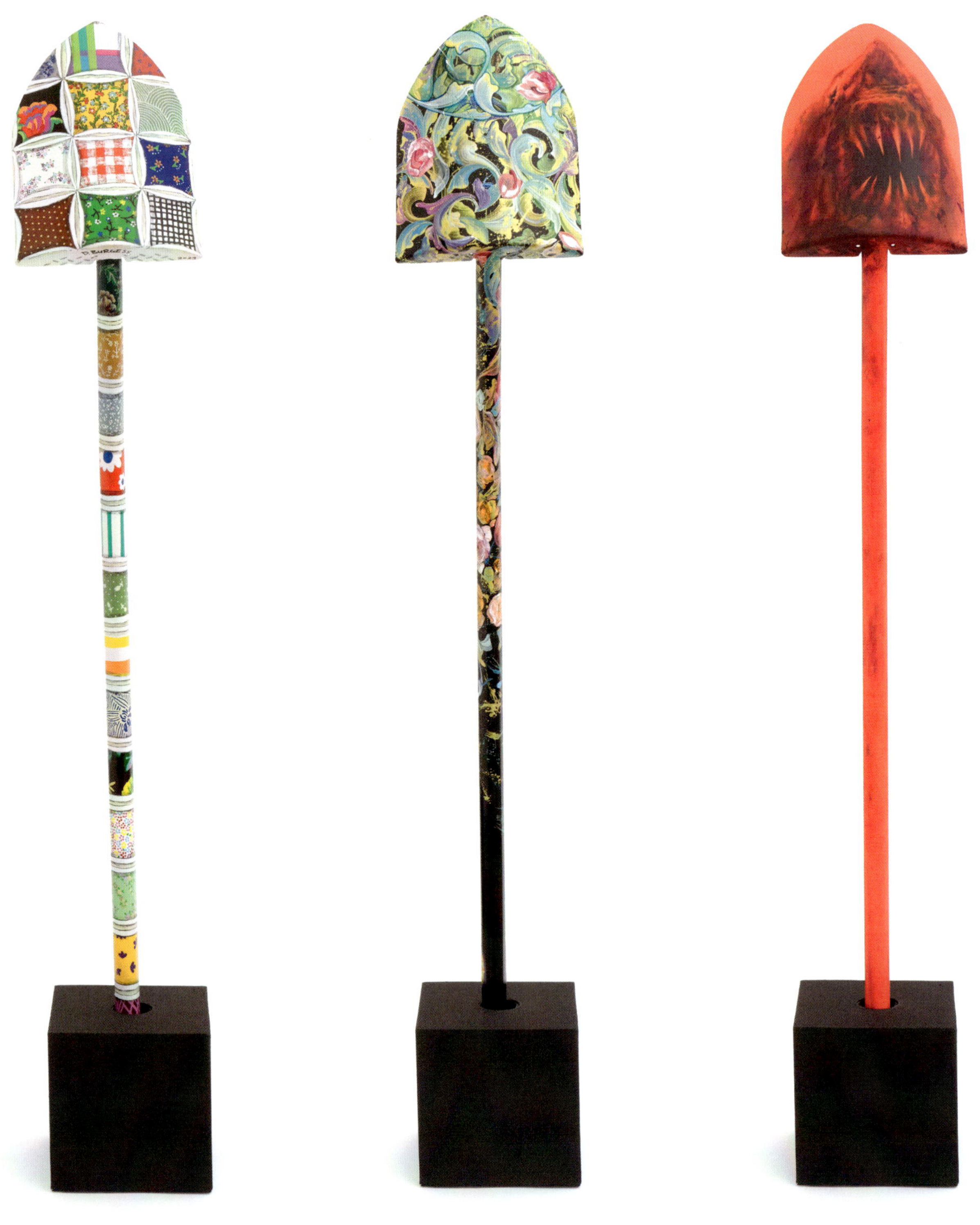

Daphne Burgess

Aiseborn

Shark Toof

     RON FINLEY

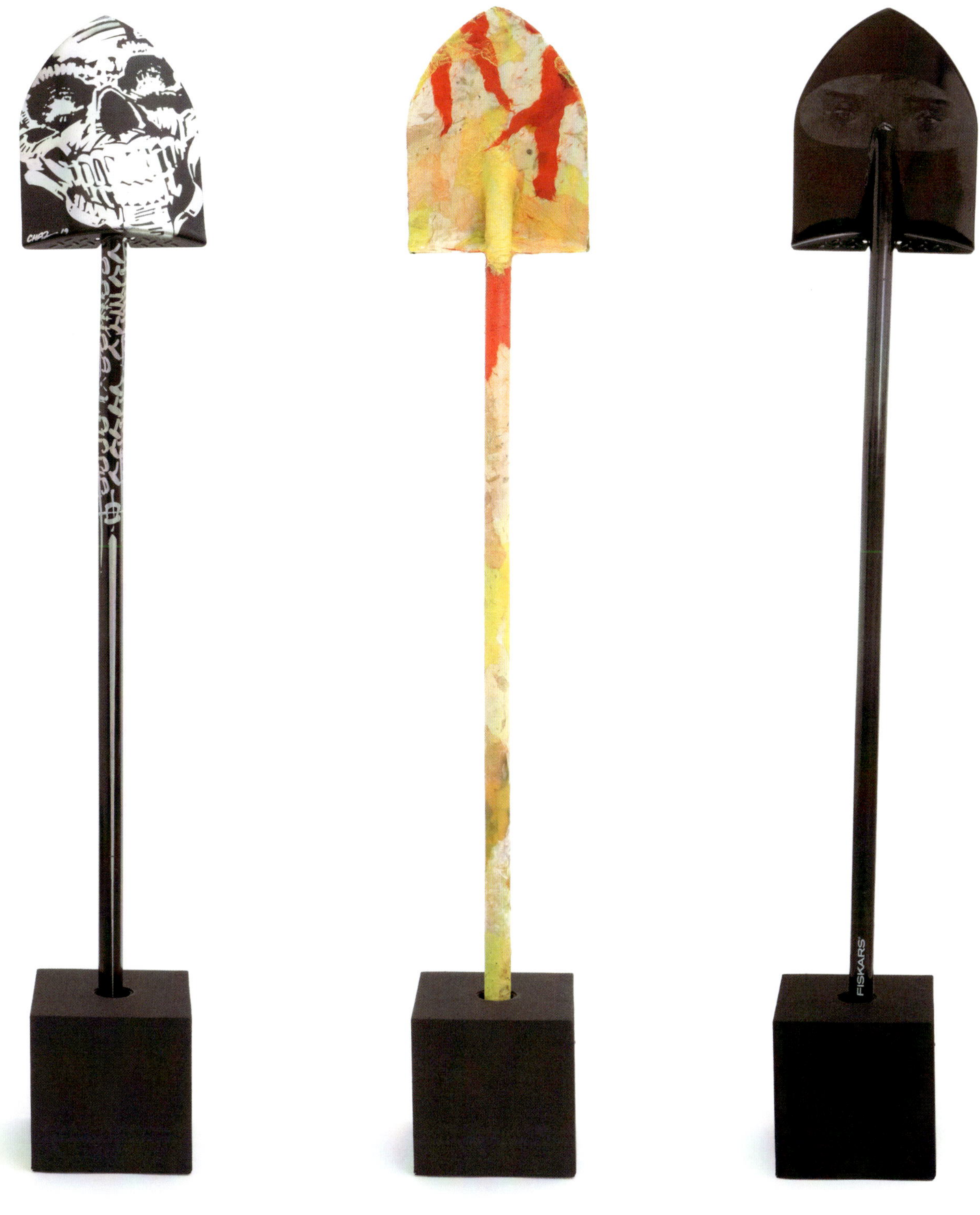

Chaz Bojórquez

Jose "Prime" Reza

Andrew Hem

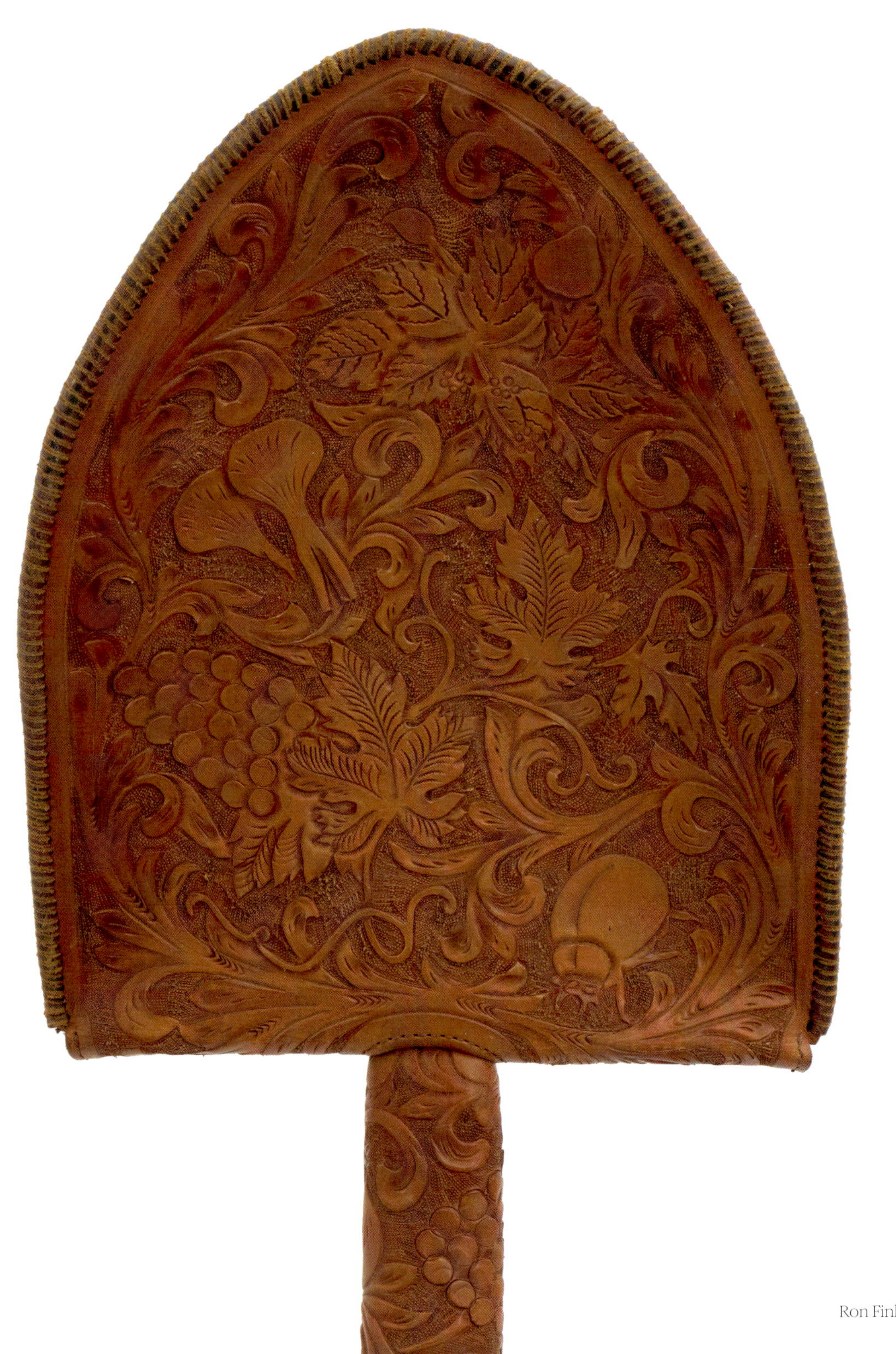

   RON FINLEY

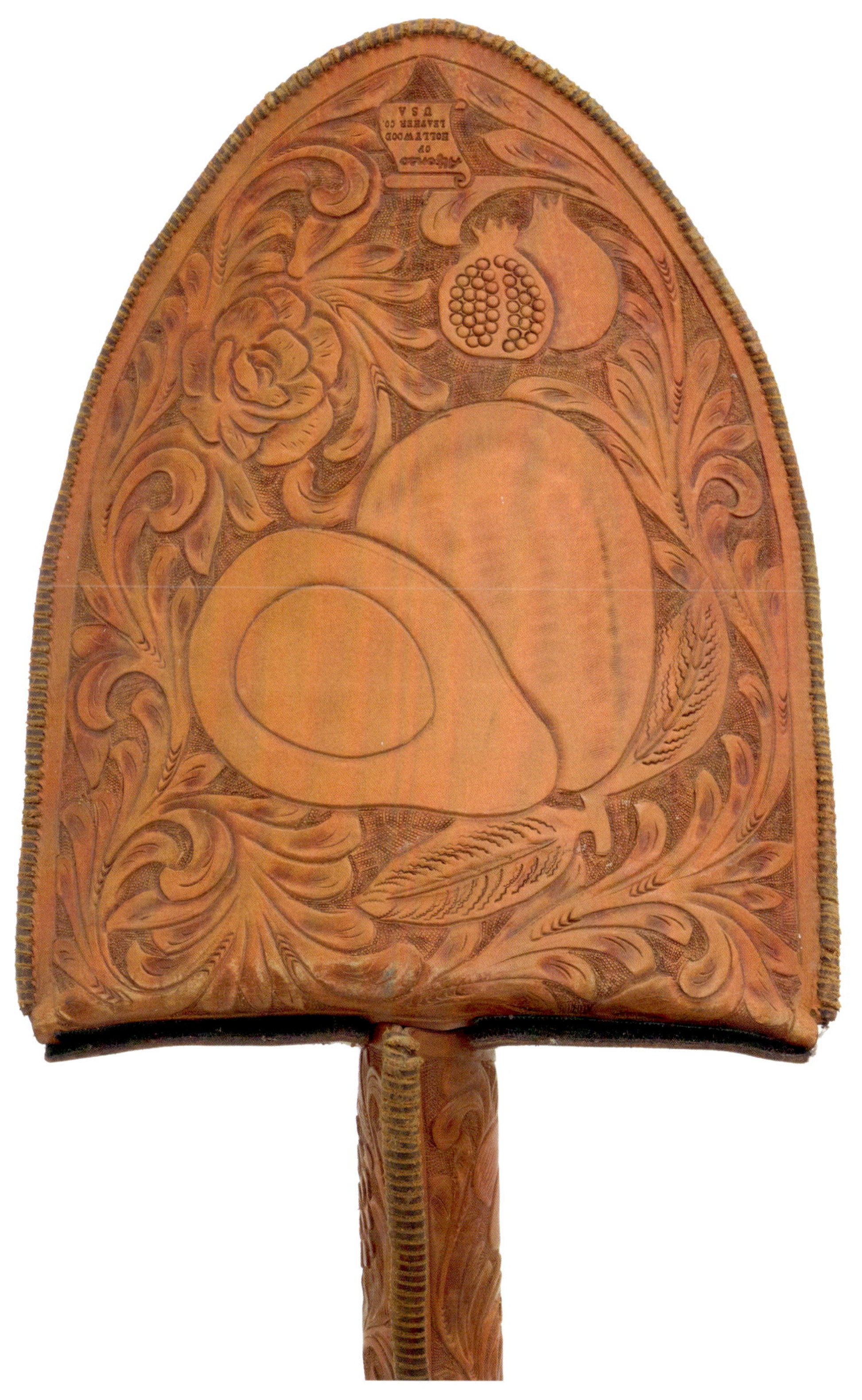

Ron Finley (back)

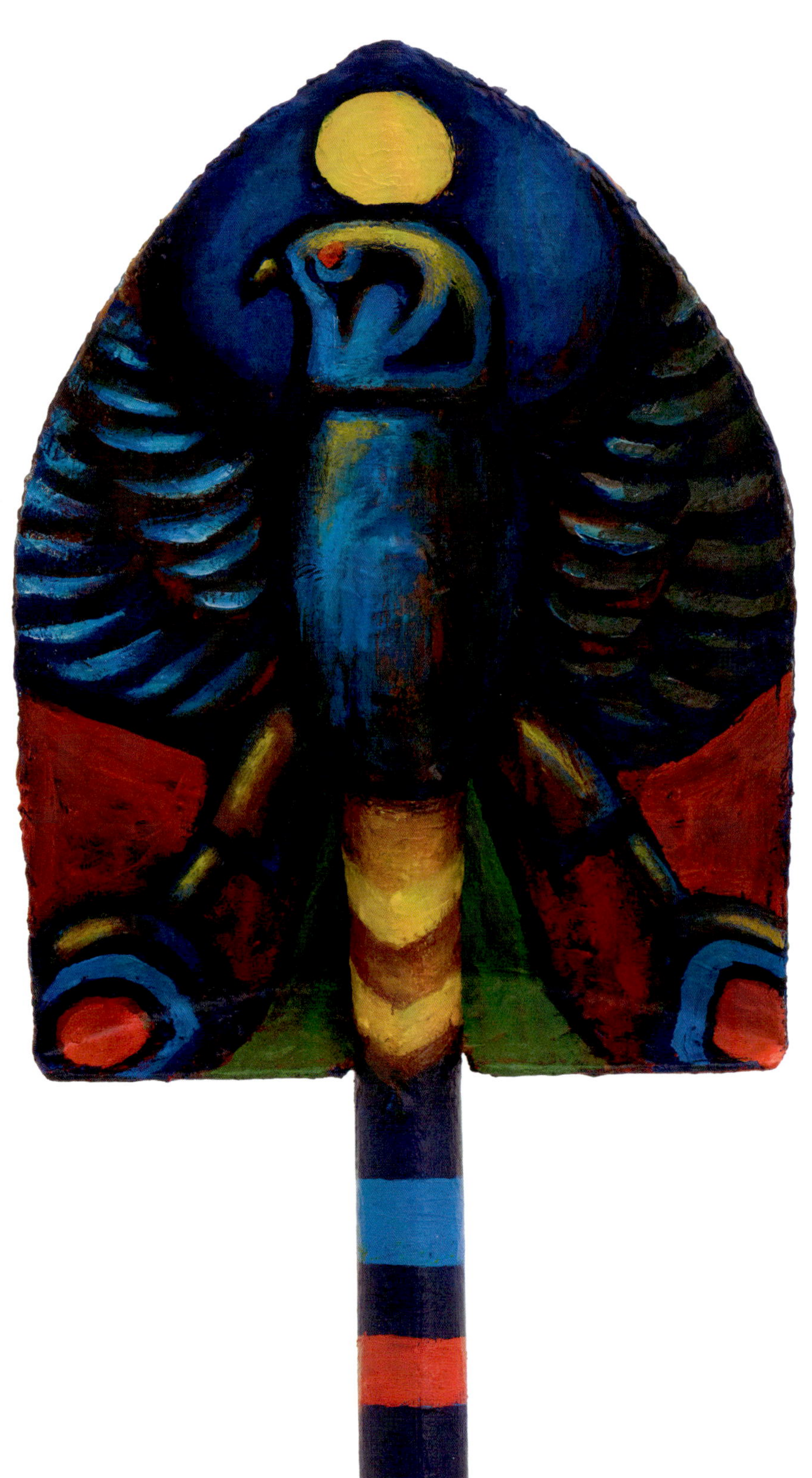

Noni Olabisi (front)

    RON FINLEY

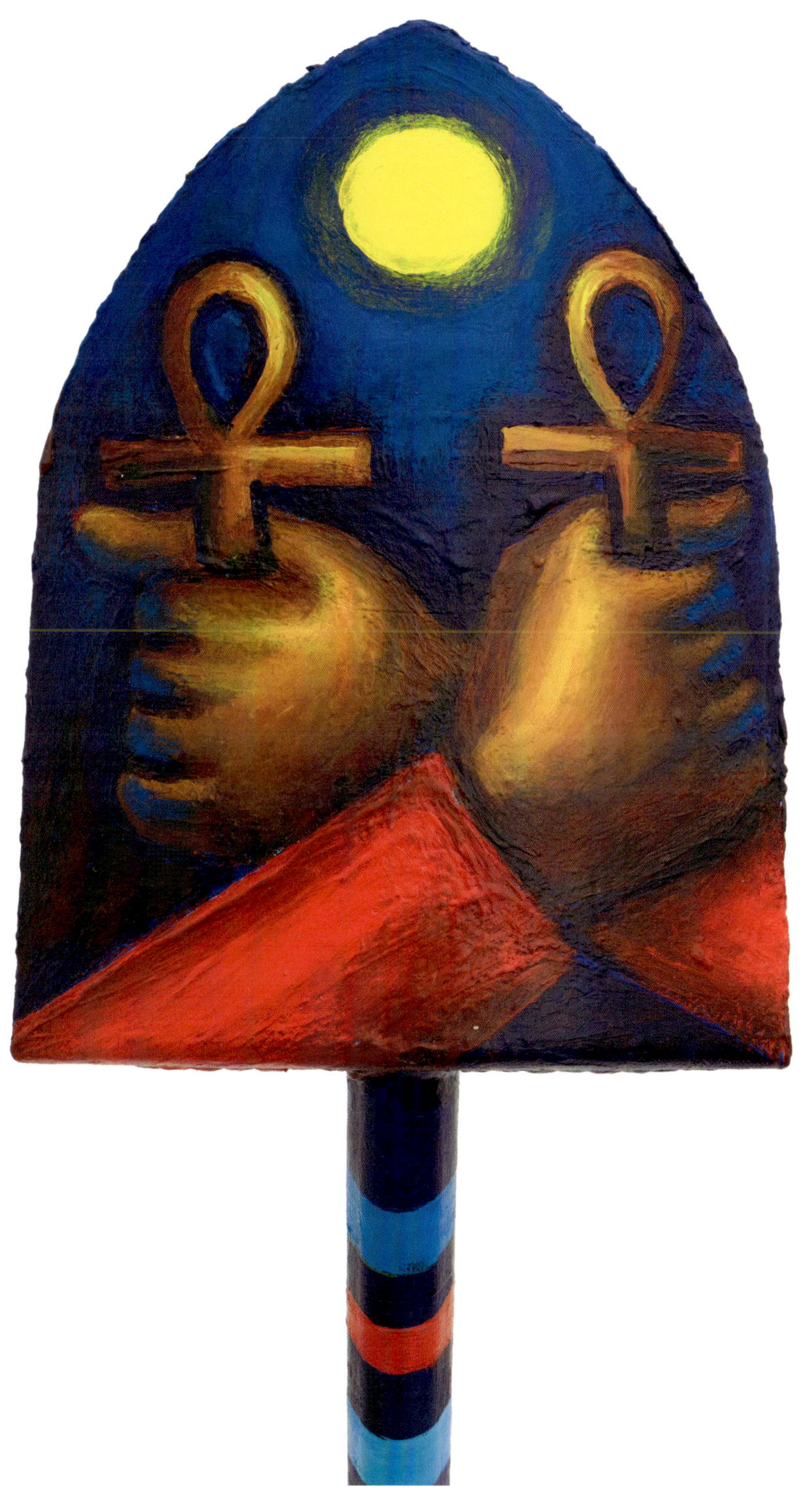

Noni Olabisi (back)

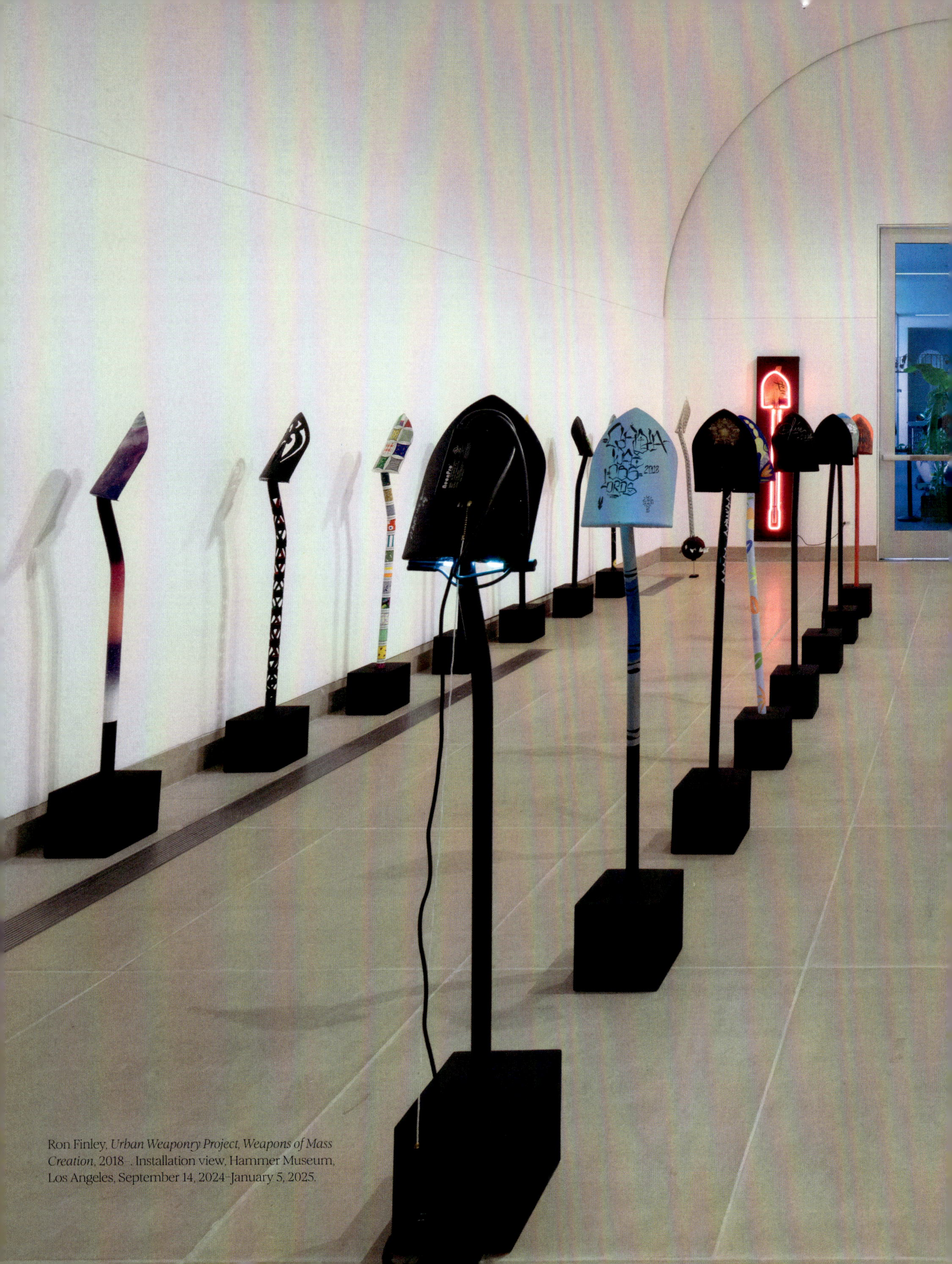

Ron Finley, *Urban Weaponry Project, Weapons of Mass Creation*, 2018– . Installation view, Hammer Museum, Los Angeles, September 14, 2024–January 5, 2025.

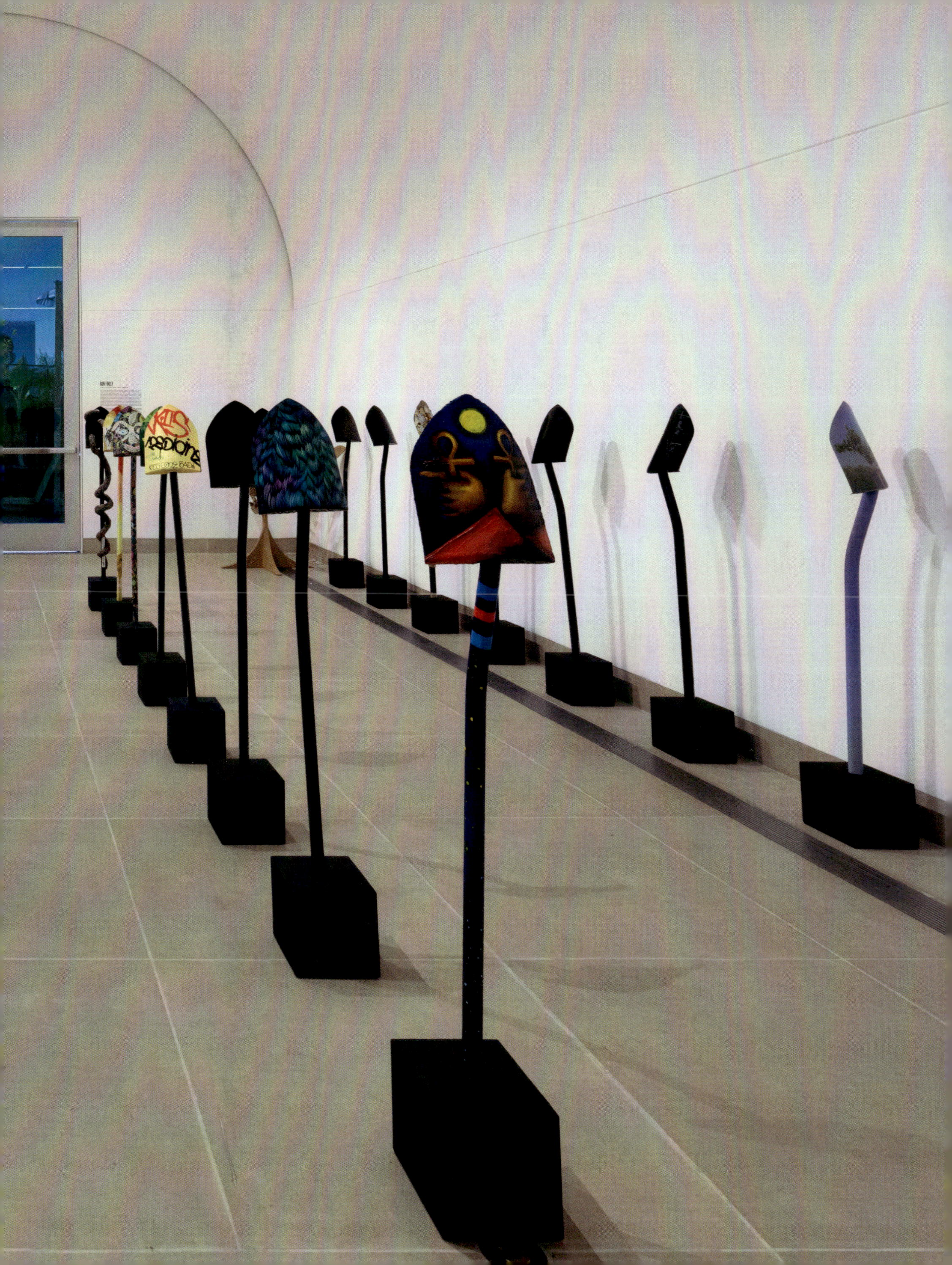

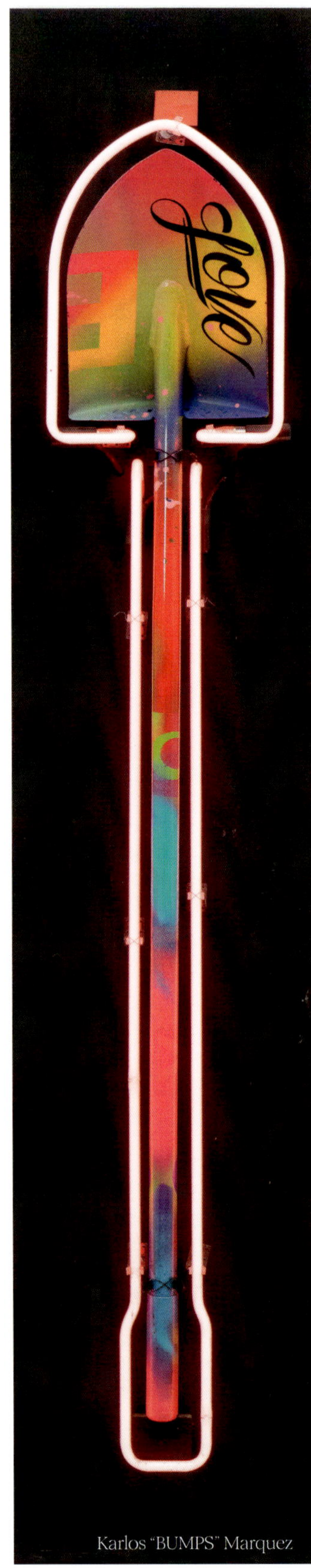

Karlos "BUMPS" Marquez

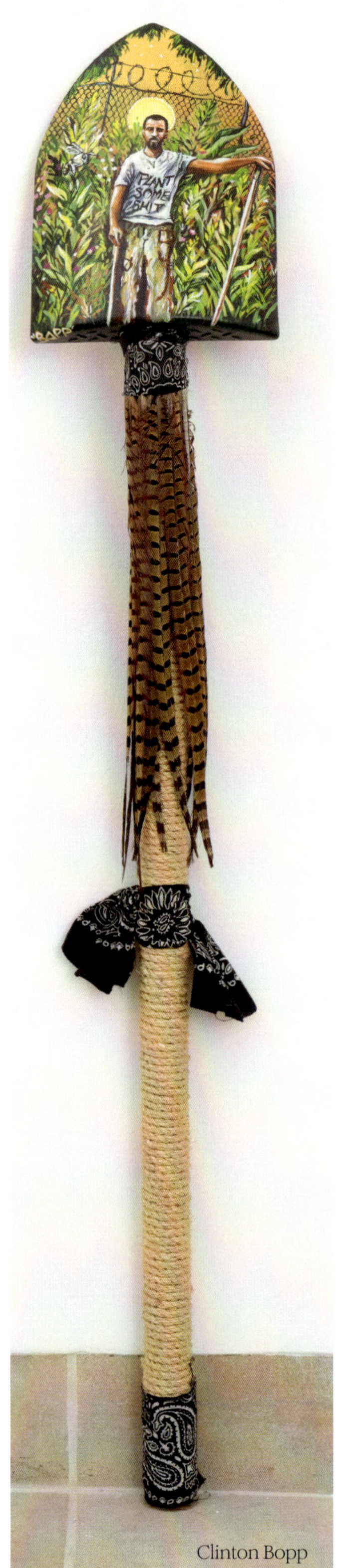

Clinton Bopp

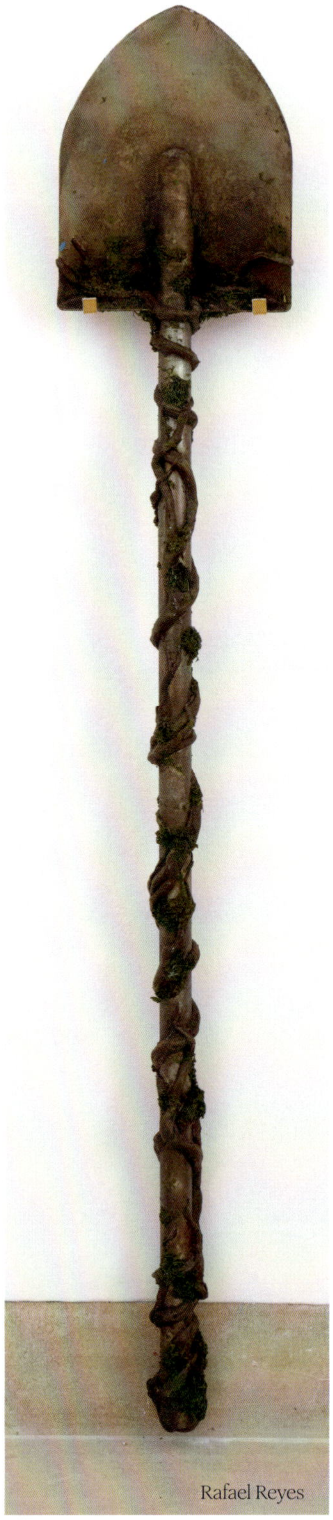

Rafael Reyes

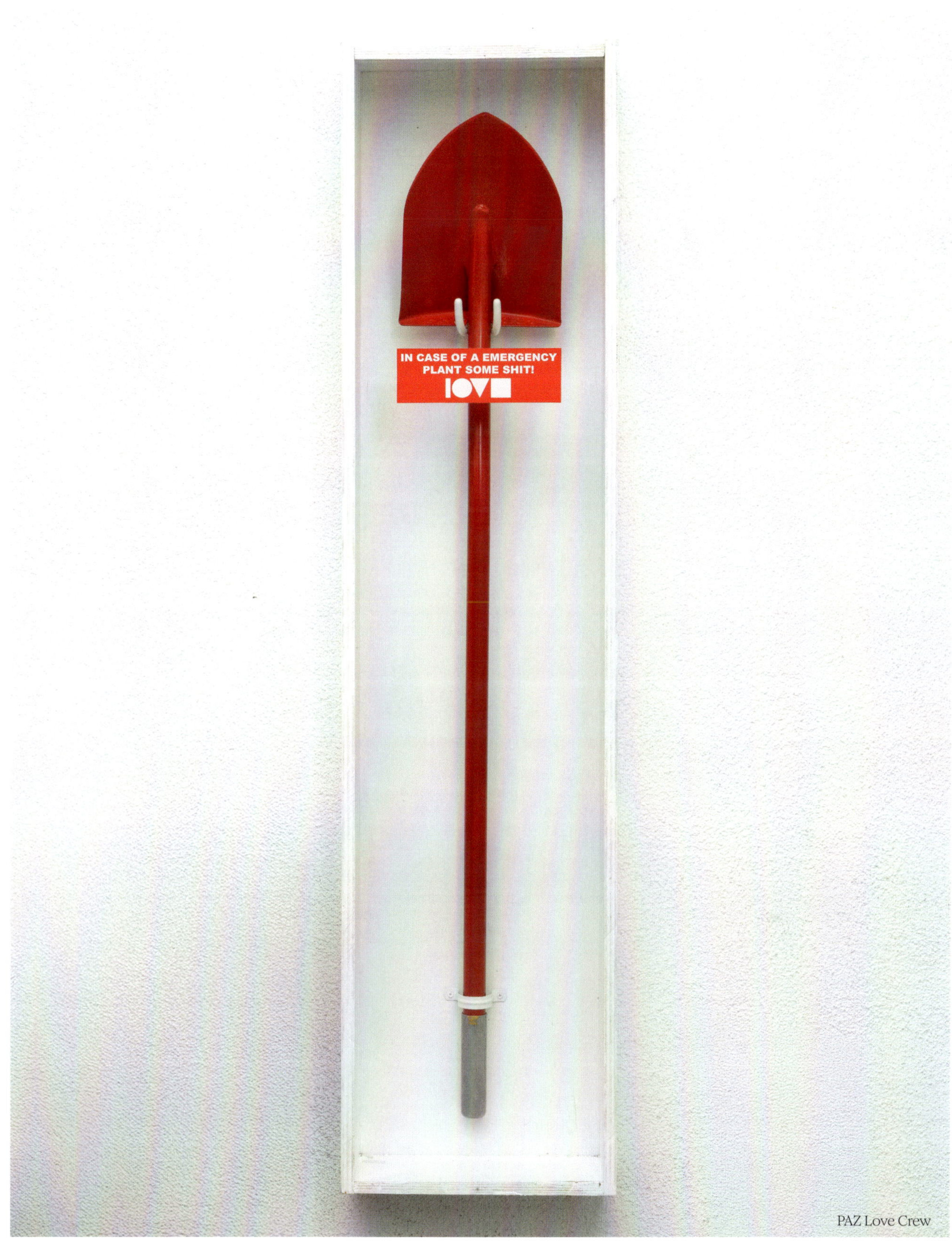

PAZ Love Crew

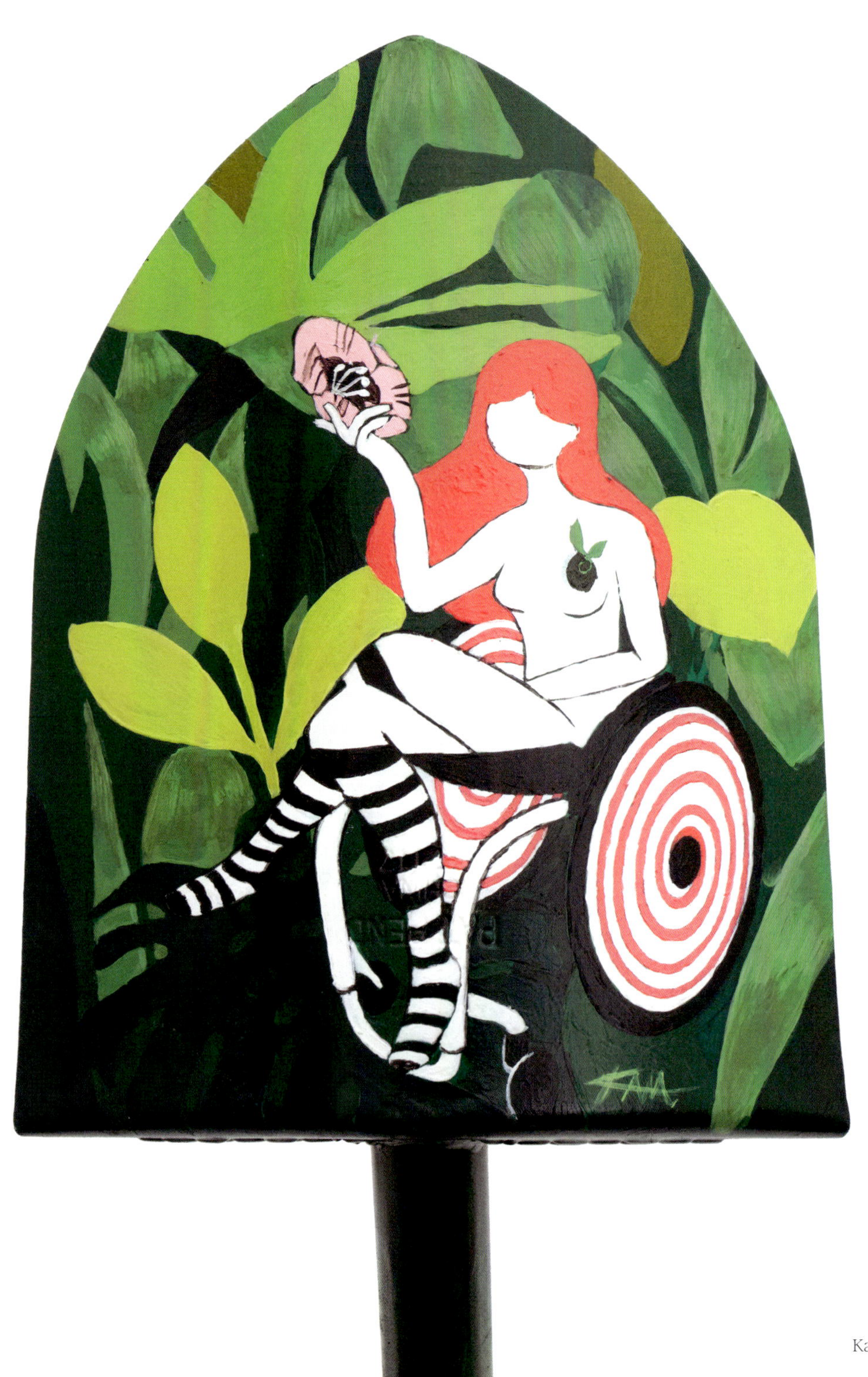

     RON FINLEY

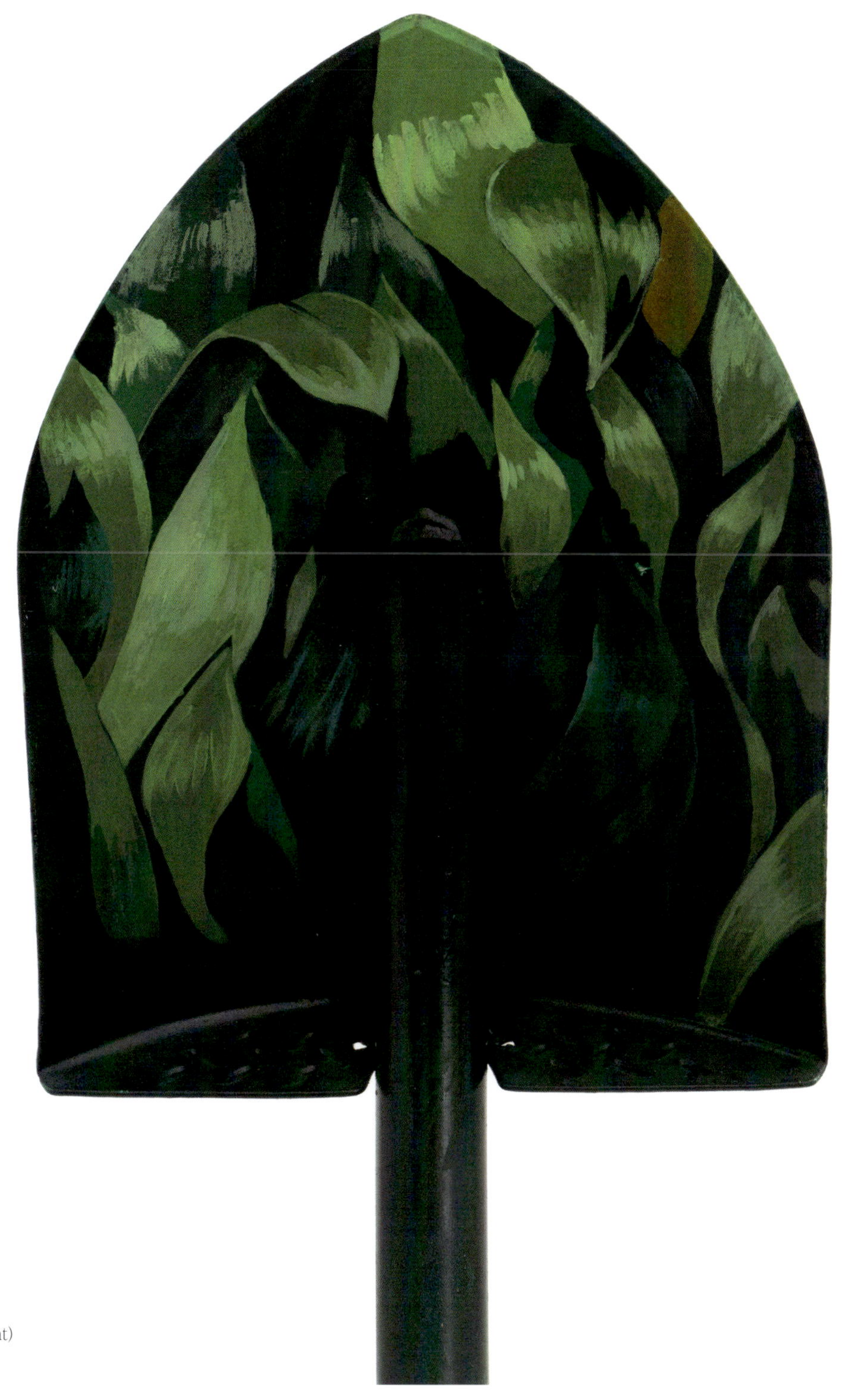

Kam Redlawsk (front)

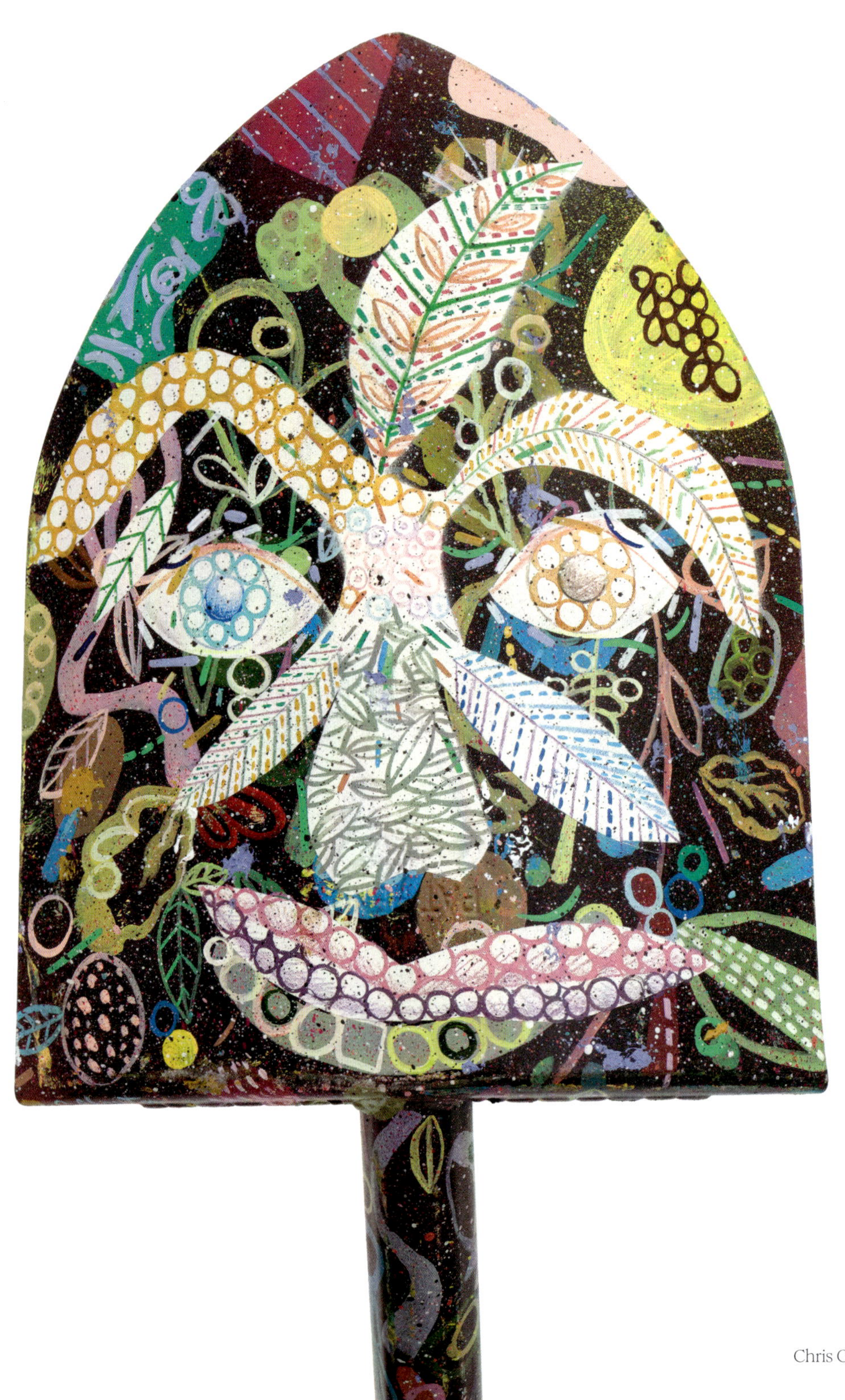

Chris Clayton (back)

     RON FINLEY

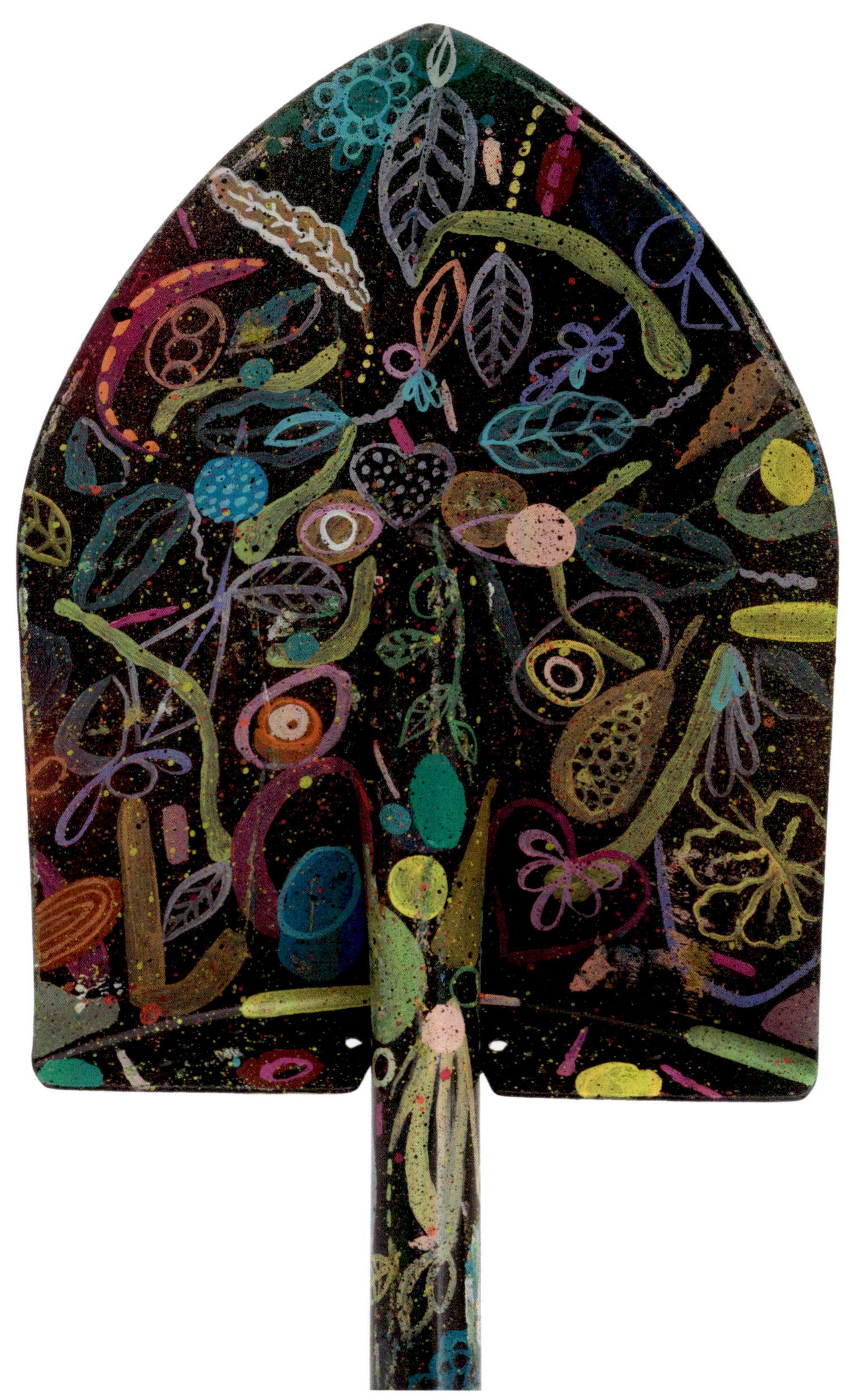

Chris Clayton (front)

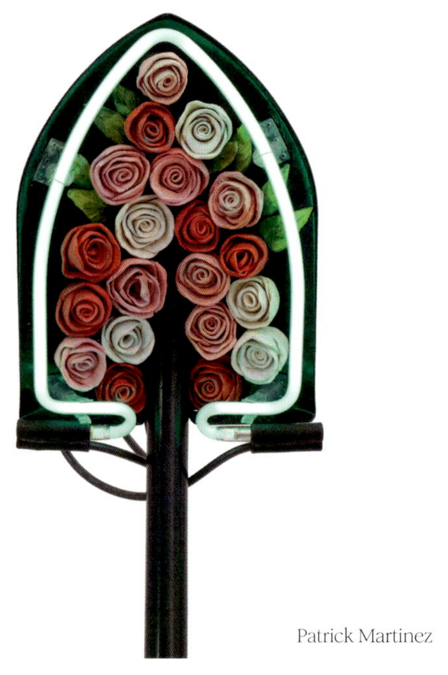

Patrick Martinez

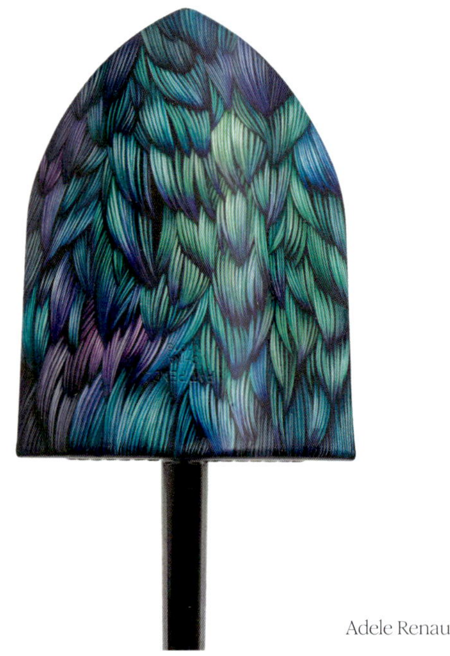

Adele Renault

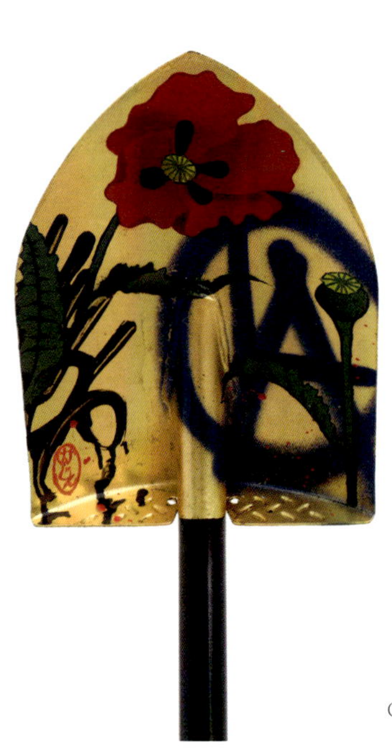

Gajin Fujita

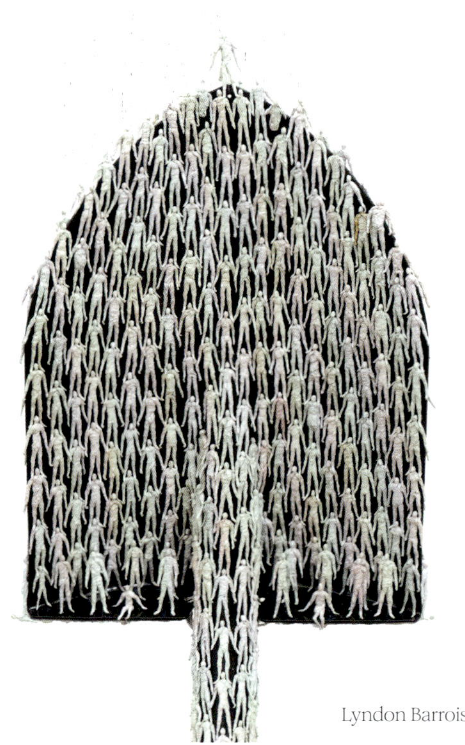

Lyndon Barrois, Sr.

RON FINLEY

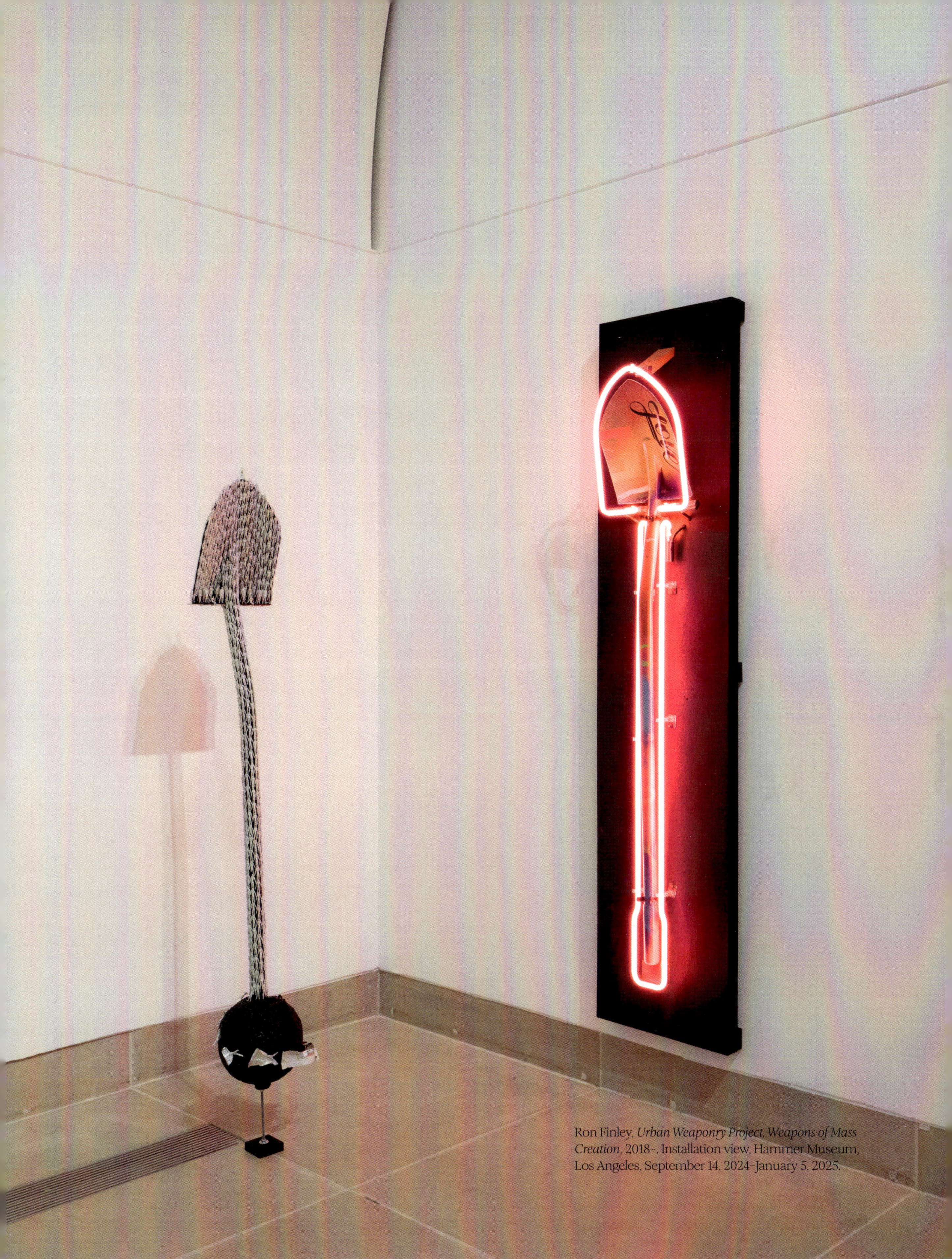

Ron Finley, *Urban Weaponry Project, Weapons of Mass Creation*, 2018–. Installation view, Hammer Museum, Los Angeles, September 14, 2024–January 5, 2025.

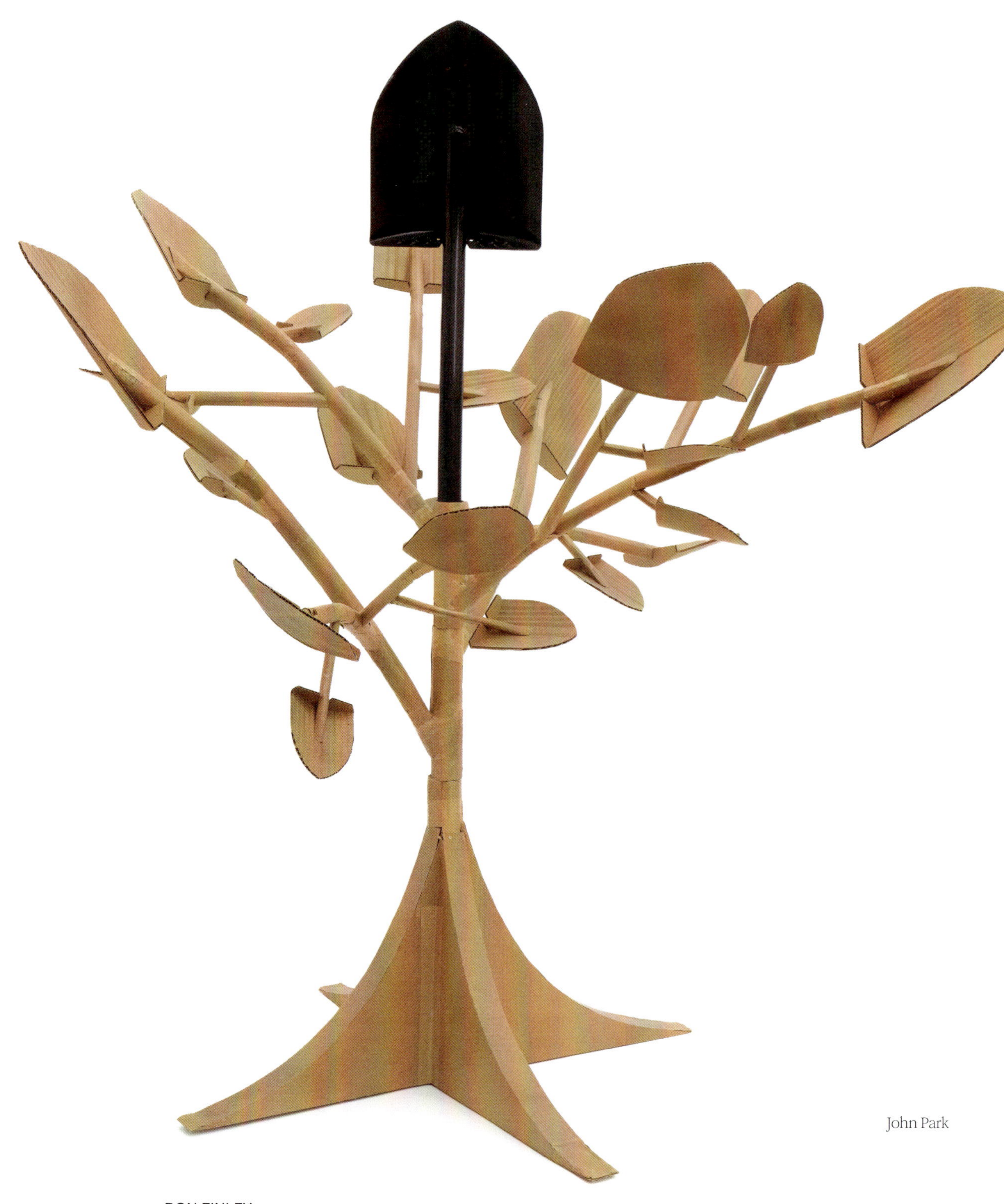

John Park

     RON FINLEY

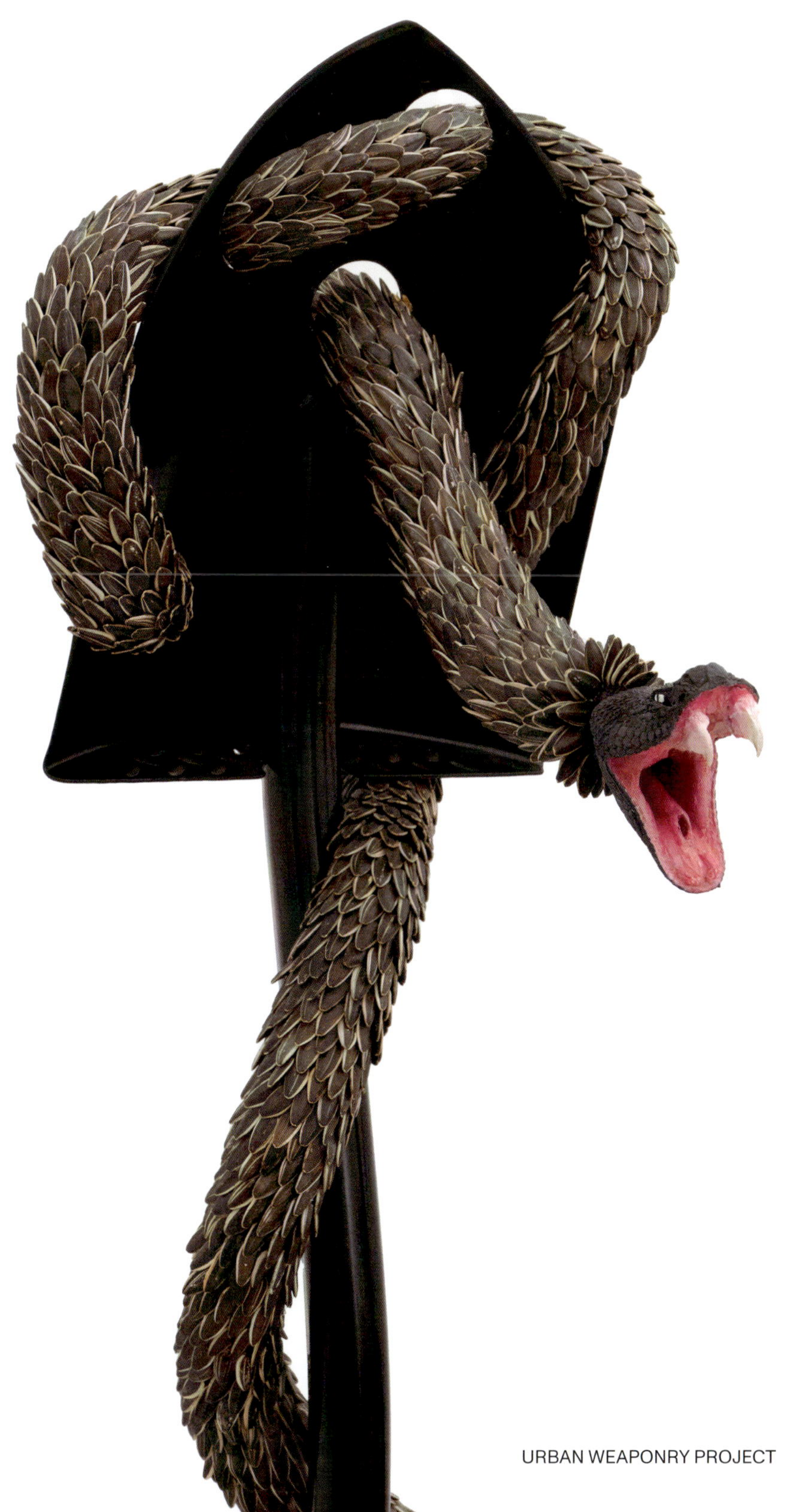

Melissa Meier

WORKSHOPS IN THE GARDEN

Good Drawing Is No Accident
Workshop with Richard T. Walsh
September 22, 2024

Artist and designer Richard T. Walsh led a workshop on drawing in the garden, teaching participants how to turn what they see into marks on paper. Walsh focused on the importance of observation and technique, drawing inspiration from a quote by the artist and educator Andrew Loomis: "Good drawing is neither an accident nor an inspired moment when the muses lend a guiding hand!" Participants practiced capturing the essence of the garden's natural beauty, gaining confidence in their drawing skills.

Dyeing with Roots and Blooms: An Introduction to Natural Dyeing
Workshop with Cayetano Talavera
October 6, 2024

Fiber artist and fashion designer Cayetano Talavera led a workshop where participants learned the art of natural dyeing by extracting dyes from madder roots and marigolds. Using resist dyeing techniques, attendees created unique patterns on cotton bandanas, experimenting with color and design to produce personalized, one-of-a-kind creations. Talavera guided participants through the process, sharing insights into the history and technique of natural dyes while encouraging exploration and creativity. By the end of the session, each participant left with a beautifully crafted bandana and a deeper understanding and appreciation for the sustainable practice of natural dyeing.

Breathing Life Into Clay
Workshop with Wayne Perry
October 13, 2024

Master potter Wayne Perry led a hands-on creative workshop where participants explored the art of working with clay. He guided them through various object-making techniques including sculpting, hand-pressing, and molding, allowing each individual to experiment with these processes and create their own unique clay pieces. Perry shared his expertise with form, texture, and technique, encouraging participants to embrace their creativity and discover the meditative and transformative qualities of working with clay.

Bonsai: The Art of Growing and Shaping Miniature Trees
Workshop with Jordan Farar
November 10, 2024

In this hands-on workshop, Bonsai Saikei master Jordan Farar taught the basics of the Japanese art of bonsai design. Farar covered the history of bonsai, discussed the types of trees ideal for this art form, and explained how to properly care for bonsai plants. Participants also had the opportunity to trim and style their own small trees, applying the techniques they learned during the session.

The Heartbeat of the African Drum Connects Us to the Earth
Workshop with Gerald C. Rivers
November 17, 2024

Master drummer Gerald C. Rivers and the Peace Player Drummers led a soulful and meditative experience, offering a brief demonstration of traditional West African rhythms. Participants were invited to join in a drum circle, engaging directly with the music and rhythm to experience the powerful communal and healing qualities of drumming.

Mosaics
Workshop with Leigh Adams
November 17, 2024

In this hands-on mosaic workshop with artist and educator Leigh Adams, participants learned to identify the best materials, substrates, and adhesives for their projects. After experimenting with a variety of tools and techniques, attendees created their own mosaic hearts, designed for display in personal gardens. Using a selection of *pique assiette* materials—such as broken ceramics, glass, beads, and other embellishments—participants were guided through the process of designing and assembling their unique creations, gaining both technical skills and creative inspiration along the way.

Wait! Let Me Catch My Breath
Workshop with Pagan George
November 24, 2024

Accomplished Iyengar Yoga teacher Pagan George led a playful and interactive exploration of breath, guiding participants through various techniques that emphasized the power of breath to transform both the mind and body. With a focus on mindfulness and self-awareness, the session explored how conscious breathing can foster relaxation, clarity, and emotional release. Pagan invited participants to experiment with different rhythms and patterns of breath, illustrating how these practices can enhance well-being, reduce stress, and unlock a deeper connection to oneself and the world around them.

The Value of Heirloom Corn:
Biodiversity, Culture, and Cuisine
Workshop with Fátima Juárez
December 8, 2024

In this workshop led by Chef Fátima Juárez, participants explored the fundamental differences between criollo corn and genetically modified corn, with a focus on the importance of conserving Mexican criollo corn and its biodiversity. The workshop covered the environmental, cultural, and social impacts of both corn varieties, highlighting how preserving criollo seeds helps maintain traditions and support the farming communities that grow them. Additionally, participants learned how to make *tlacoyos* using criollo corn dough, a traditional dish that showcases the richness and authenticity of this ancestral ingredient.

From the Ground Up
Workshop with Chris Burroughs
December 15, 2024

In this hands-on workshop led by Chris Burroughs—master composter, community activist, and founder of the nonprofit organization Garden 31—participants explored the vital role of soil in supporting life. They discovered the deep connection between soil health, plant growth, and human well-being, while learning how regenerative practices can enrich both the earth and their communities.

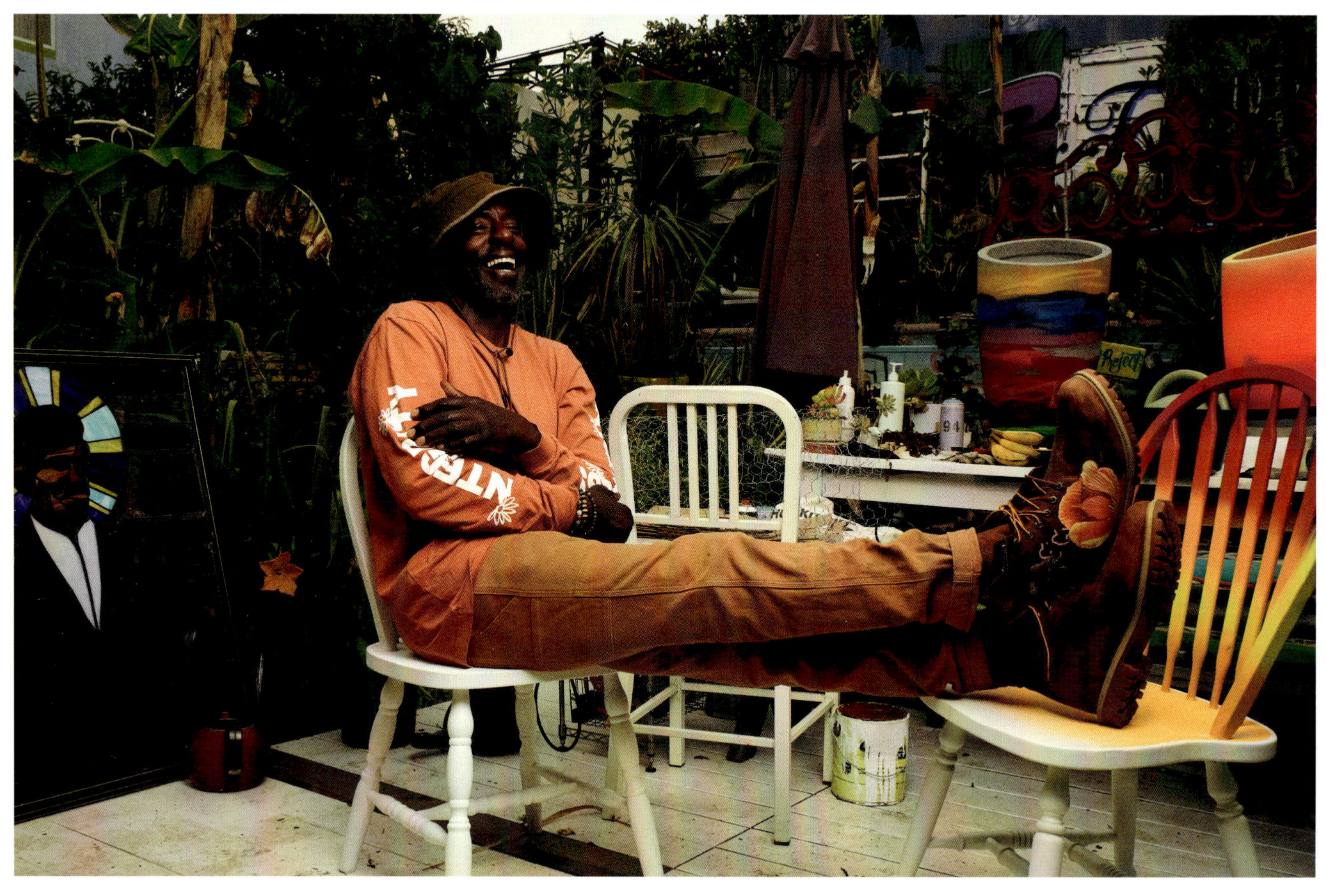

RON FINLEY

Ron Finley (b. South Central Los Angeles; lives in Los Angeles) is the founder of the Ron Finley Project, a self-described "ecolutionary," humanitarian, artist, father, and designer. Finley empowers people to grow their own food and advocates for healthy food initiatives in disadvantaged communities. He cultivates gardens in food deserts, places where access to healthy food and fresh produce is limited or nonexistent. In 2009, he began planting vegetables along parkways in South Central Los Angeles. After receiving a citation for gardening without a permit, he fought back and changed the City of Los Angeles ordinance regarding gardening on public land.

Finley has participated in group shows at the Los Angeles County Museum of Art (2022); the open-air museum Destination Crenshaw, Los Angeles (2019); and Beyond the Streets, Los Angeles (2018). He is a tireless supporter of his artistic community and has exhibited selections from his collection at the Museum of African American Art, Los Angeles, and the Booth Western Art Museum, Cartersville, GA (2012). He has lectured worldwide about food sovereignty, delivering talks on National Public Radio (2022) and as part of Time100 (2021), as well as a TED Talk (2013) that resonated with an audience of more than six million people. Finley has delivered many public lectures, including talks at the University of Southern California, Los Angeles (2022); Tulane University, New Orleans (2022); University of Minnesota, Minneapolis (2022); Purdue University, West Lafayette, IN (2021); California State University, Northridge (2019); and University of Sheffield, England (2017). The Ron Finley Project was awarded a Bronze Sustainable Development Goals Lions Award at the Cannes Lions International Festival of Creativity (2023).

This book was published on the occasion of the exhibition *Breath(e): Toward Climate and Social Justice*, organized and presented by the Hammer Museum, Los Angeles, as part of PST ART: *Art & Science Collide*.

The exhibition is guest curated by Glenn Kaino and Mika Yoshitake with Jennifer Buonocore-Nedrelow, PST Fellow.

Hammer Museum, Los Angeles
September 14, 2024–January 5, 2025

Breath(e): Toward Climate and Social Justice is made possible through lead grants from Getty as part of their PST ART: *Art & Science Collide* initiative.

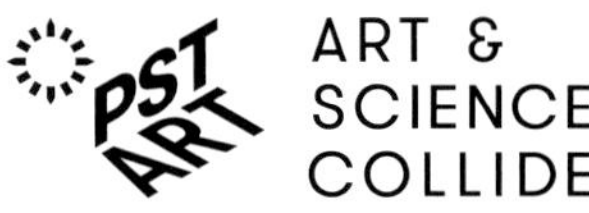

Southern California's landmark arts event, PST ART, returned in September 2024, presenting more than 60 exhibitions from organizations across the region exploring the intersections of art and science, both past and present. PST ART is presented by Getty. For more information about PST ART: *Art & Science Collide*, please visit: pst.art.

The exhibition is presented in partnership with Conservation International.

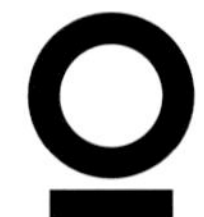

CONSERVATION
INTERNATIONAL

Major support is provided by Alice and Nahum Lainer, Eugenio López Alonso, and the Lenore S. and Bernard A. Greenberg Fund. Generous support is provided by VIA Art Fund, The Offield Family Foundation, the Fran & Ray Stark Foundation, and The Rhonda S. Zinner Foundation and Jonathan Segal. Additional support provided by Michael Silver and Amara and Alexander Hastings.

This project is supported in part by the National Endowment for the Arts.

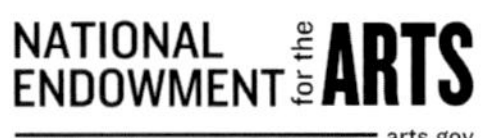

Hammer Museum
10899 Wilshire Boulevard
Los Angeles, CA 90024
310-443-7000
hammer.ucla.edu

DelMonico Books
available through Artbook | D.A.P.
75 Broad Street, Suite 630
New York, NY 10004
delmonicobooks.com
artbook.com

ISBN: 978-1-63681-177-2

Design: Polymode: Brian Johnson and Silas Munro
Copy Editor and Proofreader: Anthony Carfello
Printer: die Keure, Bruges, Belgium
Printed and bound in Bruges, Belgium

The book is typeset in ABC Monument Grotesk by Dinamo and Romie by Margot Lévêque, and printed on Magno satin FSC®, Wibalin natural FSC®, and Maxioffset FSC®.

REPRODUCTIONS
All works by Ron Finley are © the artist / Ron Finley Project. All images appear courtesy of the artist / Ron Finley Project and the lenders or owners of the material depicted.

Ron Finley is grateful to the community of collaborators whose works have become essential elements of his projects. This book features contributions from:
Ashley Rouse
Aiseborn, Painting (page 6)
Cache, Painting (pages 11, 12, 20, 27)
PAZ Love Crew, Grafitti (pages 10, 11)
Jules Maskell and Eric Nicolas, Sign painting (pages 7, 20, 23, 27)
Andrew McCarty, Shibari (page 22)
Wayne Perry, Ceramic vessels (page 73)
Pref, Painted Pot (page 73)
Ramsess, Stained glass portraits of Huey P. Newton and Bobby Seale (cover, inside cover, pages 18, 19, 20, 23, 27)
Jonathon Lew Rosado, Graffiti (inside cover, page 12)

Page 70 photograph by Dae Howerton and Dallas J. Logan. All other photography by Jeff McLane. Every reasonable effort has been made to identify, contact, and acknowledge rights holders. If there are any errors or omissions, please contact the Hammer Museum so that they can be addressed in subsequent editions.

Back cover sign transcription:
Systems must be Reevaluated
Remodeled & Reengineered,
Let's Rethink Possibilities
Reclaim recycle Repurpose!
Our lives And our Resources
instead of discarding everything
Reestablish community And
Reinvigorate Neighborhoods
Renew Purpose Renew Passion
let's Reshape & Reconfigure
Recover, Regenerate, Revitalize our health
and wellness
Restore the Soil
Resuscitate, Revive, Reawaken our planet
let's; Renovate & Rehabilitate
this whole fucked up
System

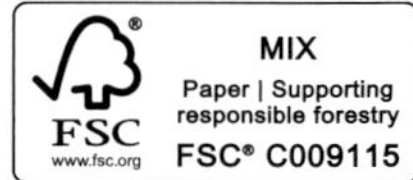

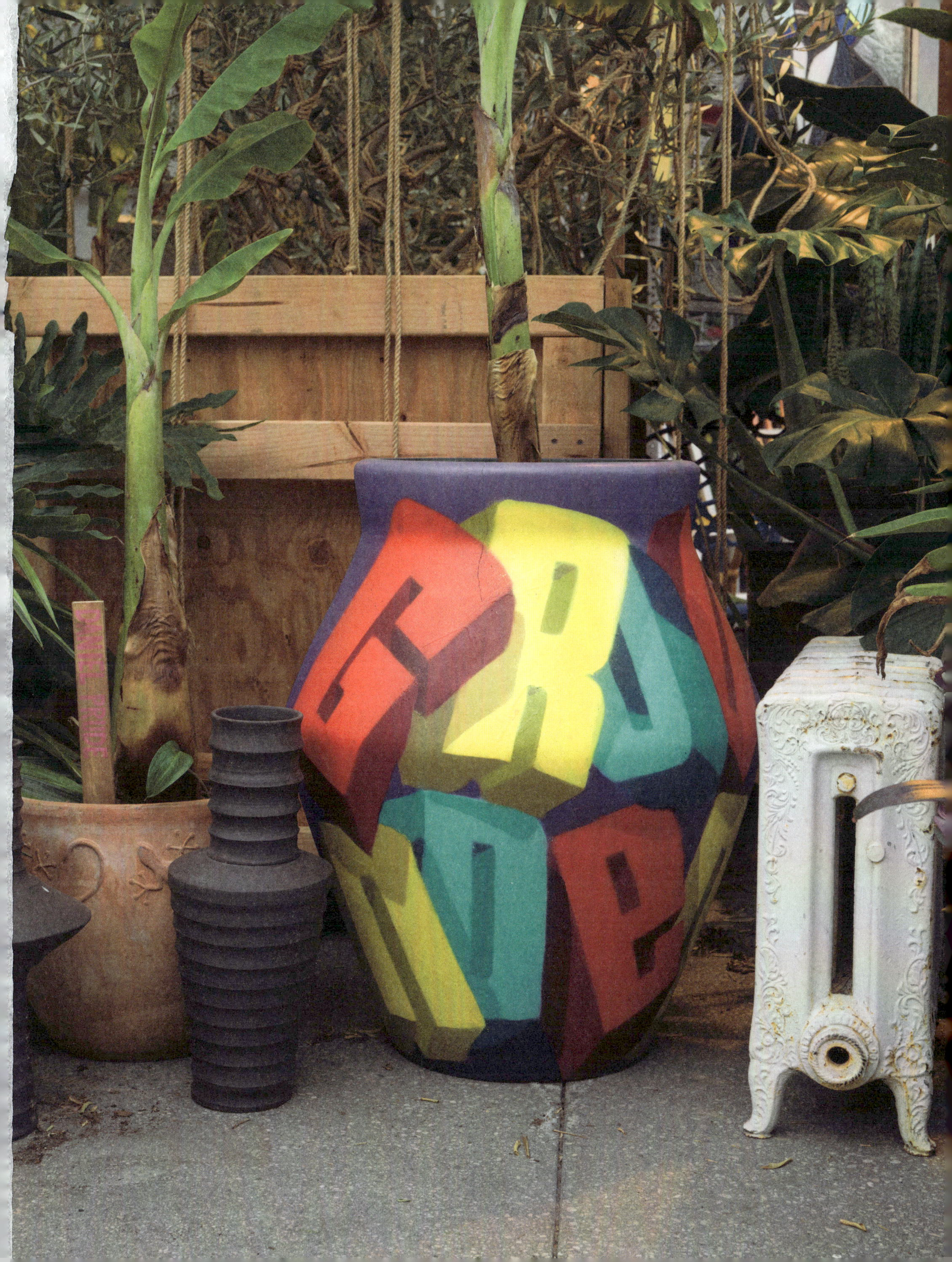

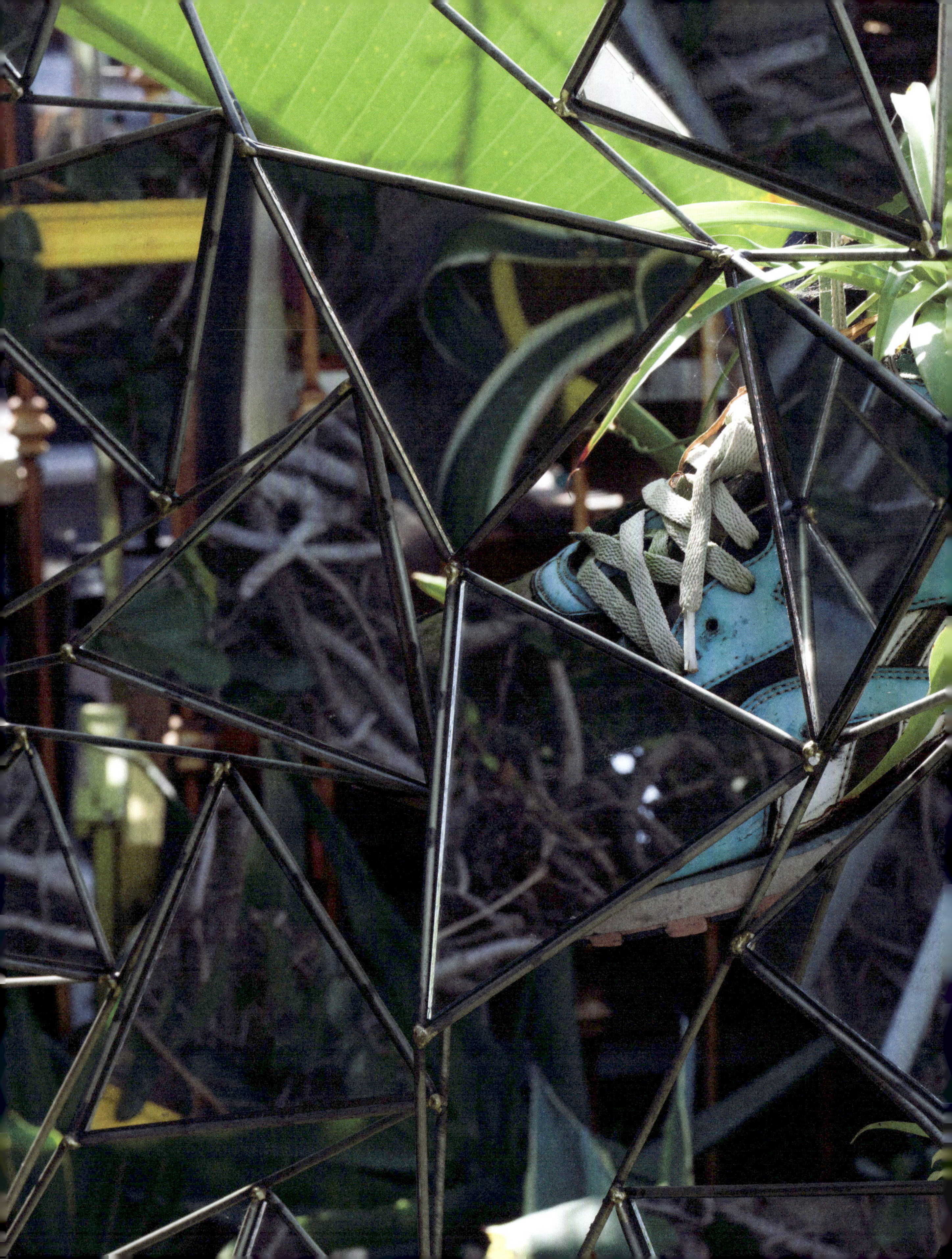